Cracking the Data Code

Cracking the Data Code

Pragmatics for Better Data Management and Governance

Richard Robinson

BEP

BUSINESS EXPERT PRESS

Leader in applied, concise business books

Cracking the Data Code:
Pragmatics for Better Data Management and Governance

Cover design by Matt Aldrich and BIGBADPIXEL Studios

Interior design by Exeter Premedia Services Private Ltd., Chennai, India

First published in 2024 by
Business Expert Press, LLC
222 East 46th Street, New York, NY 10017
www.businessexpertpress.com

ISBN-13: 978-1-63742-742-2 (paperback)
ISBN-13: 978-1-63742-743-9 (e-book)

Business Expert Press Big Data, Business Analytics, and Smart Technology Collection

First edition: 2024

10 9 8 7 6 5 4 3 2 1

For my wife and kids, for whom I do what I do, and always challenge me to imagine more

Description

Why do we continue to struggle with data? With all the powerful tools we have in processing power, data tools, and computer programming, we still search for some elusive truth to pervasive problems. AI hallucinates, "good data" that we started with is suddenly unintelligible, systems that should talk to each other seamlessly continually experience errors and need correction.

What we fail to incorporate into our data world is the fact that **data is language** and has entwined in that language its own code that does not get captured in databases, APIs, LLMs, and the systems we use day in and day out. *So, how can we crack this data code?*

By stepping back, we can incorporate the tools that already exist in applied linguistics used to crack the human language code into our approaches in how we tackle the data code challenge. Just because we call it data doesn't mean that it doesn't suffer from bias or the need for context. But by recognizing these linguistic challenges, and infusing that inside the data, we can create data code that can be cracked, data that tells us its biases, context, and purpose, and for who that data is actually useful to, and for whom it is not.

If you are interested in data, and why understanding language and jargon can help you crack the data code, this book is for you. If you've had a data challenge and have struggled to find a way to understand it, the practical foundational principles inside can help you frame your problem in a different way. And in doing so, help you crack the data code.

Contents

Acknowledgments..xi

Introduction xiii

Chapter 1   The First Book...1

Chapter 2   Communities of Practice (CoPs) 7

Chapter 3   Common Standards 11

Chapter 4   Applied Linguistics for the Layperson 23

Chapter 5   Semantics Is Just Semantics.............................45

Chapter 6   The False Premise: Everybody Needs to Know
             Everything 61

Chapter 7   Granular Data as a Red Herring........................71

Chapter 8   Practical Pragmatics—A Primer for Later 77

Chapter 9   The Failure of (How) Technology (Is Applied) 81

Chapter 10   Pragmatics in Practice 127

Chapter 11   Some Final Words..143

Notes..147

References...151

About the Author...155

Index 157

Acknowledgments

There are too many people who have influenced and supported this silly linguistics journey of mine since the first book was published. Many thanks to all the folks at Business Expert Press who provide a fantastic little publishing house for all these expert-topic books and make that knowledge accessible throughout the world on every platform and online bookstore.

I stay committed to thanking everyone I did in the first book, and the companies I have worked for—so please, if I thanked you there, I do so again here. But in particular, since the first book, Chris Day, Elisa Kendal, Lisa Taikitsadaporn, Paul Janssens, Kris Ketels, Bill Nichols, Jeff Braswell, and Hanno all have been particularly inspiring and helpful the past couple of years in trying to understand and incorporate some of the concepts I pushed forward in the first book. Chris Day, particularly, provided a robust and amazing editing job on the near-final draft. Big props to Steve Wanamaker and everything he has done with CDO Magazine in the past couple of years—he is a wonderful person and always thoughtful and supportive of the community. Big thanks to cousin Matt Aldrich of BIG-BADPIXEL Studios (https://www.linkedin.com/in/bigbadpixel/) for his cover art—he is an amazing artist. Many thanks to Bailey and the folks at Evanta/Gartner for their support of the data community and title suggestion and to the community of data folks like Pawan, Ashish, Glenn, Yogesh, John M, Doug, Peter, Alex, JoAnn, Nollie, Connie, and Moin. And finally, thanks to all who took a "beta" read and sent feedback—I definitely incorporated your input! Thanks Scott, Cody, Dmitriy, Jim, David, and Sarah.

There's Lisa I, Paul F, Paul M, Mike B, another Mike B, Mike W, Mike H, and Rich B—all who didn't get "individual" callouts last time because, well, they all share the same names! I know I've not mentioned everyone—that's an impossible task, but I do appreciate all of your support.

The team at work: Steve, Karen, Sean, Corb, Juhi, Tom, Frances, Richard Y, Bea, Pablo, Charlie, Todd, Evan, Chelsey, and Camilla, as they have to listen to me the most when the topic of linguistics or communities comes up. I appreciate the support from Marvin, Vince, Susan, Enrico, Cali, Linn, and Maureen. And of course, Jake, who's jumped head first into semantics, context, and modeling.

I have to credit the industry organizations I do (and those I do not) belong to for their tireless work in trying (and mostly succeeding) in making their community a little better off but not always getting the credit and recognition they deserve. If you are in a position with a little bit of budget, send your employees to places like ISITC NA, OMG, and X9, among others. Long term, it will be a benefit to your company, and it's a great educational opportunity and alternative reward for your people. They will learn and bring back new and innovative ideas. We need more individuals representing their communities and working toward interoperability.

To friends who are always supportive; Brian (and Diane), Lou (and Lynne), Paul (And Colleen), Keith (and Theresa) and family that have always cheered me on: Mom, Debbie and Curt, Lisa and Michael, and my fabulous nieces and nephews.

And of course, to my wife, who will walk into the back office at night or on the weekends to see what I am doing as I wrote this over the past year and during holidays. And my kids who continue to indulge their dad in his ramblings. They're all amazing people and I continue to try to match their standards. Gavin, Dylan, and Kyle—you all make me proud and I strive to make you proud every day.

Also, like the first book, these are my views, not the views of my employer or any of the organizations I belong to or represent day to day.

Introduction

Cracking the Data Code is a book about data. But what is data? Is it just numbers that provide quantifiable, unambiguous information? Is it an immutable reference source that can drive better decisions or automation through machine learning and artificial intelligence? Or is it another facade that holds so much unrealized promise?

Data is the basis for creating statistics. But then, isn't there an ongoing debate that the statistics we can show to disprove one thing can just as easily prove the same? One could argue that the data, and by association, the statistics created from that data, is pure truth. And that it is simply the interpretation where manipulation takes place.

When given the same information, why do two people interpret two different results or outcomes? Suppose we eschew data manipulation as a possibility. In that case, there is still the genuine incident that two people, looking at the same data, come away with very different, contradictory conclusions.

Let's picture an imaginary data manager that is building a model for derivatives. When working with the traders, they tell them that the price is expressed in the form of a rate. So, in building out the data model, the price field conforms to a rate as the input. When the portfolio group goes to value the positions that have been taken, however, the system errors out, as they are entering a number for the price. When the data manager points to the existing price field and what the traders enter, the portfolio group insists that is the fixed rate, not the price.

The issue here is that the traders look at the rate as the price they will be executing a swap at because the rate is changing and it determines the value of the cash flows that will occur. But as a position, that swap's rate is now fixed and not changing. The value is determined by the price in currency. The data manager is faced with two different data models for ostensibly the same thing. They could add multiple prices, like Price1 and Price2, but then when other systems need to interact with the data model, or another human pulls the data, how are they to understand which price to look at? And if Price1 is the rate, within trading systems, the data manager will need to create a seemingly duplicate field, Rate, to hold the fixed rate for the portfolio group. But, now, for a swaps trader, seeing Rate, they may expect that to indicate the floating rate such as SOFR (the secured overnight financing rate). Now the data manager must create a different field within the same data model, which is becoming more cumbersome and composed of duplicated fields. They could use aliases or class types, but now there is the requirement to manage which aliases are associated with each other or appropriate for which system or workflow.

The issue is not that the data analyst got it wrong to start—it is that two different communities look at a swap, and interact with swaps, in two very different ways and at different points. And the language they use to describe a swap is specialized and dependent upon how they interact with it and therefore diverges from each other. This is where the specialized language that different communities use, when and how they use it, and how to identify one community from another becomes important.

The reality is that data is a result of human expression and is a tool meant to communicate information. Data is not separate from written language—they are the same. I will upset many linguists here by simply stating that data is language. The nuance here is that *language* technically refers to verbal utterance versus the representation of language in some written form. So, technically, data is the same as any written language.

The difference between spoken and written language is not an insignificant nuance. In spoken language, it is possible to emphasize parts of speech to alter meaning. In cases where the speaker and listener can also see each other, other nonverbal cues can influence the expression and interpretation of speech. Recorded language, written down, in books and documents loses much of what spoken language conveys.

The fascinating thing when we transition to *data* is that most data proponents would argue that removing those mitigating factors present in spoken language is a benefit—removing potential ambiguity and manipulating what should be the *pure* data definition. That is, many data professionals would argue for the removal of the influences of utterance (especially in reported speech) that may introduce context or inferences not originally intended. They would also enforce or remove specific clarity in direct speech otherwise conveyed by nonverbal cues that would not be present in written language.

There is a belief that a data professional or a computer scientist can impose some level of control or order upon the lexicon they define and those who use it. As we shall explore, this is one of the primary failings in understanding that contributes to the continued confusion around data, standards, and creating reasonable data solutions.

When I first started getting into *data* things over 25 years ago, I felt a missing simplicity and certainty. Data is data. It has a specific meaning. In time, I began to notice the nuance of data and how semantics (and later context) could be the key to unraveling the data misinterpretations resulting from nuance. I still did not grasp the complexity of language.

Machine Learning and Artificial Intelligence efforts have an underlying assumption that these machines can parse and understand the data we feed them. Semantics are a vital tool in this. But semantics alone cannot solve the issue of data existing as a representation of spoken language. Semantics alone does not solve the problem of speech being removed from the nuances of tone, emphasis, inflexion, and other cues that can potentially alter the meaning of collected data. Semantics, especially, cannot account for the inherent biases of the sender of data (i.e., the speaker) and the receiver (i.e., the listener).

Furthermore, spoken language itself is not free of problems. We all have been on the wrong end of miscommunication and misunderstanding at one time or another. Whether it was traveling internationally and giving a thumbs up or OK hand signal in Brazil (both insults), or misinterpreting a significant other's request for doing *something special* and making dinner at home instead of reserving a table at the new hot spot; jargon, dialect, and bias all can cause communication to go awry.

There is a good cartoon where a scientist is looking into a small office and appears confused. Behind him, another scientist walks up, with a Labrador retriever on a leash. He tells the confused scientist "I told you we'd give you a big lab!"

The negotiation between two speakers that results in the process of repair* and accommodation highlights that misinterpretation, such as

---

* I will apologize in my first book, I incorrectly referred to "repair" as "fixing."

with the big lab, occurs regularly in spoken language. It is well known that spoken language can be misinterpreted and result in confusion or ambiguity. So, finding fault in the data world is difficult when the solution is assumed to remove such ambiguity and confusion through the rigor of data definitions and structure.

Applying this method, in my work with data scientists, architects, and computer scientists, we continuously run up against the barriers described above. Whose definition is correct for any one term? Why is it so difficult to communicate across domains? What in applied linguists can we define through a Communities of Practice (CoP)? Why wasn't disambiguation working at scale?

This work inevitably led me to a seemingly straightforward investigation. I googled "semantics." While I have been using the term "semantics" for two decades, I never really went further than scratching the surface of the basic definition that semantics gives clarity of meaning within a context. I found a rabbit hole leading me to linguistics; Chomsky, Saussure, and Mencken, among others. Then further into technical crossovers like Langefors, and sociolinguists like Labov and Wegner-Treyner.

What I discovered is that I did not have an excellent appreciation of semantics at all. Nor did I appreciate the role linguistics and applied linguistics should have with the data profession. Further, looking at data through this newly coalescing lens, I saw that I was not alone in wearing blinders. Data professionals, standards creators, subject matter experts, regulators, operations, and senior level management all might have some sense that there was something in language that was important, and focus on tools and technology as the ultimate solutions that would create order out of the chaos.

I now occasionally come across a data professional, ontologist, analyst, and even an algo trader who has a linguistics background. But they remain the exception rather than the rule. There is a challenge of eyes glazing over when *linguistics* is even mentioned. Linguistics and applied linguistics sound very abstract and tend to turn people away. So, if you have picked up this book, and have gotten this far, I thank you and hope I can make the topic more accessible, and illustrate its relevance to data and even applicability in everyday functions.

My goals in the forthcoming chapters focus on the complexities we deal with in data, and therefore language, and how we can utilize even the basics of applied linguistics to overcome some of the core challenges we come up against and dispel some myths and misunderstandings about data.

What I hope you get out of the coming chapters is a sense of the journey I have taken in my understanding of linguistics and data, and the new lens we can all use to enhance our skills. I will reintroduce applied linguistics, and expand upon concepts, from a layperson's view, setting the foundation for you to build upon. We'll consider the major themes impacting data professionals—and those that rely on data (yes, you, technologists)—such as context and bias, but also those not explored such as the over-reliance on semantics and technology. We will examine the major technological themes from data storage to Large Language Models. Finally, I'll offer the application of the linguistic concept of pragmatics as the next stage in trying to solve the problem in data that has challenged us since the dawn of the technology age.

That is, how do we crack the data code using linguistics?[†]

[†] Many thanks to the Evanta/Gartner conference folks who first came up with this title for a presentation I gave regarding my first book.

CHAPTER 1

The First Book

When I wrote "Understanding the Financial Industry Through Linguistics," I reacted to what I saw as the paving of a dangerous path by regulators and some standards proponents. Moreover, the assumption is that those not directly involved with the nuts and bolts of day-to-day data have little understanding of data and meaning. There is a vision of a gilded yellow brick road composed of homogenous standards that will magically create transparency and wipe away the complexity that plagues attempts to rationalize financial communication.

The basic argument that still permeates many industries is that the multiple existing standards and (financial) languages act as a barrier to better transparency and regulation and impose real economic costs. Haldane stated clearly in 2012 that "The economic costs of this linguistic diversity were brutally exposed by the financial crisis."[1]

We should not ignore linguistic diversity as a real issue. Linguistic diversity is a primary cause for many problems, and ignoring this fact indeed can be pointed to as a primary factor in the 2008 financial crisis. For that matter, language diversity is at the center of significant political, economic, and social issues. Wars and cultural elimination programs have language diversity as a critical component of their genesis.

However, the resulting dialogue regarding "a common language" that followed Haldane's work did not explore the linguistic issues regarding diversity in language, even if he and others tried to steer in that direction. Instead, the focus was purely on the assumed conclusion that diversity in language is the issue and, therefore, we should remove diversity.

Ignoring for the moment that this conclusion puts forward a solution ahead of understanding the problem, the proposed solution misses the reality of language and the basic tenets of linguistics. Further, it overreaches what the definition of a "common standard" implies. The envisioned solution aligned with a technology-centric approach to data and data management without any linguistic basis.

My goals in "Understanding the Financial Industry Through Linguistics" were to provide an essential background and understanding of what the "financial industry" means, to give a foundation of relevant concepts from an applied linguistic perspective, and to bring these together to analyze standards efforts and regulation. Throughout, the point was to examine why certain things are the way they are, regardless of how irrational they might seem to someone on the "outside," and why attempts at change across the industry have been ineffectual.

Further, the typical friction points in any industry (the points where miscommunications occur) are where two diverse groups interact. Commonly we point to silos as prime suspects in fostering poor communication, protectionism, and lack of transparency. Yet, from a social point of view, silos can be viewed as individual Communities of Practice that share a common culture and language in support of a shared goal or function. The fault proscribed to silos is that they are a foreign culture, purposely being protectionist against change or outside influence. We do not see the resistance to adopting external data standards as a language issue but as a simple change management challenge and cultural protectionism.

A key issue is that, on the whole, most laypeople do not believe there is a problem with understanding data and standards. Data, and by association, standards, are seen as universal and common. There is a common belief that something is a standard endorsed by a repu table standards organization, a creation through rigor, inclusive of all necessary experts, and free of influences. Unfortunately, this is not the usual case. Lack of participation and support by companies (cost and the time of letting employees volunteer their work) means that standards efforts are woefully underresourced. And this leads to bias, perception, and expertise issues. These issues, I hope made clear, were not an indictment of standards organizations but rather a misunderstanding by those adopting standards about what a standard is, what it means, and how we should evaluate it.

Everyone brings their own bias and experience to bear when creating, manipulating, or in some way using data. We naturally are prejudiced to assume others share our perspectives, how we perceive data, and the terms we use to describe data. This extends to the standards creation process. Yet, we ignore all of these human aspects of language in evaluating data and standards.

Through a Community of Practice lens, I brought forward that CoPs will have their own specific language, whether simply a nuance of dialect or jargon or something more linguistically significant. The challenge, then, is when communication needs to happen between CoPs—there is a natural friction on which CoPs' language (i.e., data and data definitions) is the *right* one and which is the *wrong* one. This goes further in cases where CoPs with a level of power of influence seek to impose their definitions and language upon other CoPs.

This is very much the state of things regarding regulators and the data-related regulation they look to impose upon those they regulate. There is a significant effort on the side of the regulators to try and understand and work with those they regulate. Still, when an impasse occurs, typically over the understanding of data or processes related to data creation, the most common default position is for regulators to enforce their view and definitions—using something anointed as a *standard* as the proxy for what is *right*. There is no regulator maliciousness, but in a sociolinguistic sense, regulators understandably will be conservative—that is, they will mistrust those they regulate, lest they be misled or hoodwinked through obfuscation or misdirection.

Standards have been held up as some mystical thing that automatically transcends all understanding to create a "common understanding" or a single universally accepted way of doing something. In other words, enforcing standards is expected to remove the opportunity for wrongdoing. Again, regulators cannot be immediately at fault for instinctively believing that defaulting to a "standard" as a solution is the correct path.

Yet standards, especially data standards, are still written language expressions of a particular community. That is, any standard necessarily is created in and for the language of the community making it. It is impossible to expect a data standard to be representative and applicable to many diverse, though interconnected, groups of CoPs. Nor is there anything in the property of a standard that can prevent all misinterpretation or result in a universal common understanding.

This data standards challenge is primarily a language issue. The cultures of different CoPs drive this issue. Misunderstandings and confusion due to language differences tend to be blamed not on the language differences but on the natural friction between cultures that causes distrust. Language barriers complicate being able to overcome this distrust.

The issue of language difference does not just exist between regulators and the regulated. CoPs, being groups that share a common culture, function, and purpose, exist through any industry in a messy overlapping set of Venn diagrams that I had for the financial industry, expressed as interconnected cubes.

Though this interconnected web exists in all industries, I focused primarily on financial services. Within financial services, we can break COPs across multiple axes (see Figure 1.1), whether front, mid, and back office, by asset type (equity, fixed income, etc.) or even business type (broker, investment manager, etc.). In other industries, you could have factories and suppliers or the splits between a newsroom, print media, and showrunners in a media enterprise.

CoPs exist within a social system that their joint work helps to support—such as financial services or the manufacturing industry as a whole. These social systems are often mistaken for homogeneous systems where we expect sameness as the rule. However, in reality, social systems are messy, heterogeneous mixes of cultures, processes, and languages that all work (mostly) in concert to complete the larger goals of that system while simultaneously working individually within their respective CoPs on specific, seemingly unrelated goals.

The core connecting thread within social systems remains the data —there will always be data that crosses lines between CoPs. Data is like the lifeblood through the many different organs of a living system, each organ is akin to another CoP performing a specific function, sharing that lifeblood of data but changing it at each interaction, using

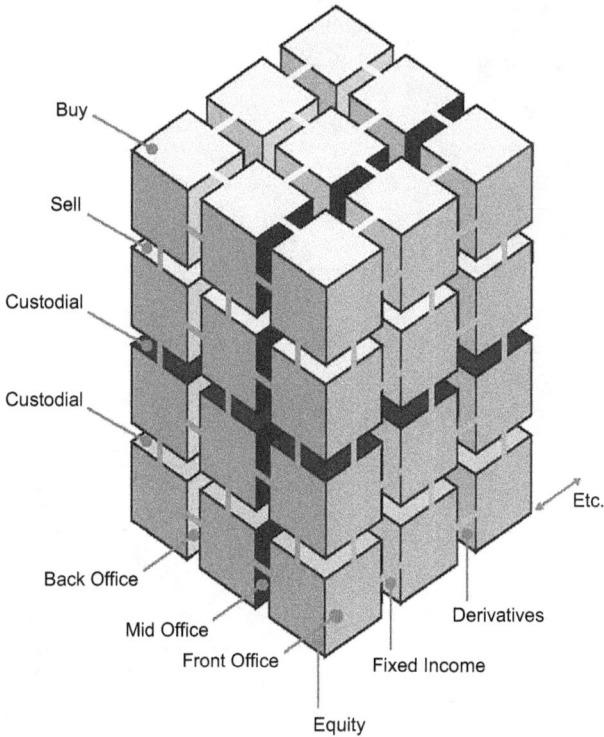

Figure 1.1 Communities of practice matrix

it in different ways, for other purposes, and different individual ends, even if together they are supporting the same overall system.

The key finding of the first book is that there are many diverse component communities within financial services, with language across those communities being just as diverse. Further, accepting and understanding these diverse, overlapping, and competing communities is only a first step to grasping their language differences and setting the stage for a better understanding of the relevant data. Finally, the imposition of common standards alone will not solve the problems that the industry and regulators must solve. The challenge of data in any industry has a basis in language and social systems, and those issues need to be part of any foundation of future solutions.

The single truth is that there is no single truth.[*]

---

[*] Credit Steven Meizanis.

CHAPTER 2

Communities of Practice (CoPs)

I covered Communities of Practice (CoPs) in extensive detail in the first book. Anthropologists Jean Lave and Etienne Wenger coined the term while studying apprenticeship as a learning model in the 1991 book *Situated Learning*.[1] From a linguistic history perspective, it is a relatively recent concept—although, arguably, social scientists have used variations of the concept for analysis for years. Etienne and Beverly Wenger-Trayner have spent the decades since that 1991 book exploring this study area in more detail.

Initially, this chapter you read was further down toward the back of my planned outline. But as I looked back, I kept referencing CoP throughout each chapter. No surprise, as CoPs are central to the theme of cracking the data code mainly because each CoP encrypts the data code that needs cracking!

Etienne and Beverly Wenger-Trayner have a website[*] that has been an indispensable resource, and I do pull significantly from it for references. To start, "Communities of practice are formed by people who engage in a process of collective learning in a shared domain of human endeavor."[†] However, not all communities are CoP—nor is every gathering of people that share an experience a CoP.

Let's explore what exactly I meant by that statement. First, in looking at the domain aspect of a community, something like your LinkedIn network may be a community, but it is not a CoP. All the people in your network may belong to the same CoP, but your network itself is not a CoP. "It has an identity defined by a shared

---

[*] Accessed February 16, 2023, www.wenger-trayner.com/introduction-to-communities-of-practice/.
[†] Ibid.

domain of interest. Membership therefore implies a commitment to the domain, and therefore a shared competence that distinguishes members from other people."[‡] But, we need to combine this with the process or practice —that is developing a shared set of tools, procedures, or otherwise—that is ongoing and has commitment from members to engage and continue to contribute.

So, just because a group shares the same interests—such as science fiction movies—doesn't make them a CoP. And one individual's interest in science fiction movies wouldn't mean they belong to any larger group of people they don't know or interact with that share the same interest. This group does not constitute a CoP even if, individually, they are experts, know every line and event in *Star Wars*, and all read the *Star Wars* Wookiepedia.[§] Now, if they interacted and were active contributors to the Wookiepedia or held meetings to discuss and analyze their findings, creating new and unique learnings and methods for understanding the *Star Wars* universe, this rag-tag group would begin to look like a CoP (they are active participants and practitioners in the specific domain they share).

Interaction and learning together are essential. I am not a member of the CoP of applied linguists. Regardless of all this research and writing and new (I hope) learning I am creating through this book, my previous book, and my published articles, I am not participating in joint community work in the applied linguistics world. Even if I attain a high level of expertise in this subject, unless I am participating and jointly working with others in the domain of applied linguistics, I am outside of that CoP and simply looking in. That is to say, you can be an expert in something, yet not belong to that CoP.

Further, many experts collaborating to share their knowledge isn't necessarily a CoP. Innovation, the creation of new knowledge, and solving problems are vital activities. All members don't need to agree; universal agreement usually doesn't breed new ideas. Active discourse is a crucial ingredient for creation and innovation, including optimizing existing processes, and is a primary indication of a robust CoP.

[‡] Ibid.
[§] Accessed February 16, 2023, https://starwars.fandom.com/wiki/Main_Page.

Finally, a CoP is enduring. It's not a project group that gets together to build a product and goes off on its way. It's not a study cram session for the semester. A CoP doesn't need to formally meet together constantly, but it is some ongoing entity. They don't need to interact together directly, but their joint work creates the community. So, traders and trade assistants in the front office don't work together directly across the industry. Still, their collaborative efforts contribute to a more significant body of learning and new work practices that create and impact the front office CoP.

CHAPTER 3

Common Standards

The great thing about standards is that there are so many.
—Tannenbaum

Interpretation of meaning is a vital part of language. When using overly broad or generic terms, there is a significant possibility for misunderstanding. When we discuss *common standards*, what exactly is meant by this term? Someone can be very conservative with the interpretation at one end of the spectrum, applying the concept to particular conditions or a well-defined use case. For example, if one needs to hang a picture on a wall, she will look for a picture hook. While there may be various picture hooks, you wouldn't use one for another function. I've become partial to the super hook style, a metal loop that goes into the drywall. But there are the traditional J-hook, command strips, the Claw, heavy-duty hangers with three-pins, screw hangers, and push-pin types. But at the end of the day, all of these can only be used for hanging things, as opposed to any other function.

We can use some standards for different needs at the other end of the spectrum. EXtensible Markup Language (XML) is an excellent example, with an application for various purposes, from building websites to creating documents to organizing datasets. Depending on an individual's perspective, we can reasonably understand whether the interpretation of *common* is comprehensive and meant to apply to anything and everything.

By using concrete examples, we can begin to see that the narrower, more conservative meaning applied to *common* likely has a more appropriate use in regards to standards. Fasteners are an excellent example. In this context, fasteners refer to all types of screws and nails, as opposed to staples, push pins, picture hangers, or paper clips of various shapes and types. One could argue that simplifying fasteners would provide much-needed relief to consumers confused by the thousands of existing options. It could save significant money regarding confusion, delay, misuse, incorrect purchases, and manufacturing retooling.

For an adherent to the broad meaning of a *common standard*, they could reasonably question why both screws and nails exist. And why there are different types of screw heads, from Torx to flathead to Phillips heads. For simplicity's sake, why not agree on a single common standard that eliminates nails and standardizes screw heads around one single Torx version—specifically indicating the metric versions versus Imperial, or even simplifying it all to one single screw head, regardless of size, application, or torque requirements?

For someone who is not a subject matter expert in the use of fasteners (such as myself), there is little understanding of the impacts of material type, environmental conditions, strength requirements, and so forth when selecting a fastener. So, without real expertise, a nonexpert with minimal knowledge of the multiple nuances and mitigating factors could believe simplifying the options is a reasonable way of thinking.

The truth is there needs to be multiple different standards and types for fasteners, that correspond to the various conditions and required uses. This standardization implies a certain level of required expert knowledge and the influence of the use case and context.

The reality is that multiple factors come into play that affect the use case and need in choosing the appropriate fastener. Environment, materials, intended use, and regulated requirements are all part of the equation. It should follow, then, that standards for data should be no different—that within any single industry, many factors can impact the meaning, intended use, and utility of any fragment of standardized data. Language adds further complications—as any data are subject to the intrinsic properties of being language.

When taken to an extreme, this line of reasoning for a single common standard—to use one single type of screw for all applications—probably seems pretty ridiculous, and admittedly, it is intentionally exaggerated and hyperbolic. So what should be considered a *common standard* for fasteners? The reality is that this pivots on the linguistic opaqueness of the meaning of *common*. When applying this lingual ploy to something physical (e.g., fasteners), the proposition that having one single screw replace all the variety of fasteners globally within the construction industry should be absurd to the reader.

Dogs Are Arbitrary

If a single term or word has too many limitations, what about focusing on a *concept* that we could prescribe some universally accepted meaning? Even if we use different words or definitions, a *concept* could arguably transcend the issues that using pure terms or definitions inherently invokes.

Take the arbitrary word *dog*. What *dog* represents could be described as a four-legged, omnivorous mammal with canines for teeth and generally kept as pets, but not wholly. As a concept, *dog* can represent a kind or class in a linguistic sense.[*] But a class or kind concept infers further hierarchical representations instead of genuinely being some Chomskyan version of universal grammar where all society shares the same conceptual meaning of dog.

Further, in a sociolinguistic sense, different Communities of Practice (CoP) will have different interpretations of any agreed, supposedly universal, conceptual meaning of dog. A CoP focused on hunting will have a vastly different interpretation of what qualifies as a dog versus a CoP involved with herding, support, or companionship. Many dog clubs do not allow or consider mixed-breed dogs. And let us not forget there is a scientific definition of a dog.

So, what is a dog? While the generic concept of *dog* can provide some level of central anchor to provide further granular attributes, those general attributes and their importance quickly vary depending upon the CoP involved. In other words, what one person in one community may think of as a *dog* can vary from what someone in another community may consider a *dog*.

The attributes any hunting CoP may require to describe a dog's properties will diverge from those a CoP focused on companionship

---

[*] Accessed August 16, 2022, www.ncbi.nlm.nih.gov/pmc/articles/PMC3607366/.

would deem important. Breed types may be introduced as proxies to assist with descriptions, but individual attributes may disqualify any specific dog, even in these cases. A Beagle may fit the role of the hunting CoP, but that breed may just as well have (different) attributes that qualify it as a companion instead and be wholly unsuited to hunting requirements.

Breed classification, to be fair, does satisfy the needs of a specific CoP regarding the genealogical classification of a species based on physical attributes. Yet these classifications do not provide enough granular specificity regarding attributes related to appropriateness for use cases such as hunting. While generalities, such as temperament, can be prescribed to various breeds, these are gross generalities that do not persist universally. Some may be environmental, affected by training, rescued, abandoned, or brought up in a city versus a farm. Other factors may be genetic or otherwise innate in an individual. Many Dalmatians are deaf due to overbreeding, but this cannot simply be assumed due to the primary classification of that breed, and over time, it may not apply at all. The species classification also may not disqualify that impaired individual from its ability to have a place in the use case of something like a hunting CoP.

First, *dog* as a general concept is not suited to determine if any instance is useable or appropriate for any specific CoP. We know it is a dog, as a concept. Still, no indicators provide any utility in determining suitability for any purpose other than distinguishing it from different types of animals (except, perhaps, wolves, coyotes, dingos, hyenas, and the like). Furthermore, the attributes required to determine if any particular dog would fit a hunting CoP are also wholly unsuited to deciding if that dog would fit any other CoP. In data terms, the taxonomies a data practitioner would use to model either instance would be completely different.

That is, providing an individual with the data that the *concept of dog* encapsulates does not give a hunting CoP member enough information to determine fitness. So, the data are insufficient. If I enhance that data with other granular information, such as that it is attentive, responsive to commands, and gentle with children, this additional data, while applicable for companionship, would still not provide any further insight for a hunting CoP.

The taxonomy needed to describe a dog depends on the CoP, and specific use case, rather than some overall common model for describing a dog. Proclaiming it is a German Shephard or Irish Wolfhound, in addition to the other details, does not illuminate. Yet, if I instead state that the dog can flush out birds and then retrieve any that I shoot—the breed status, attentiveness, responsiveness to commands, and temperament with children have little or no relevance. The data that are important for one community are different than the data necessary for a different community, and even *shared data* carries different weight, definition, and relevance.

In standardization, one could argue that all potential attributes of dogs should be identified and captured for all individual animals. But what does this gain versus the costs and practicality of doing this? Our data requirements expand and explode rapidly, with conflicting requirements. Furthermore, it does nothing to empower individual CoPs in managing the data (e.g., the attributes that CoP finds relevant to their identification of a dog) required to be assembled, analyzed, and utilized for decision-making processes.

First, you must gather all the attributes each CoP finds important. There will likely be some overlap in attributes, though their individual level of importance will vary by need and use case by CoP. The qualities conveyed by any particular attribute will also have variability, so we need to make further accommodations to align these. Definitions of data—how they are phrased, or interpreted—will differ, even if they are thought to be *common*. A dog's coat, for example, could be viewed in terms of appropriateness for water versus allergies or vacuuming.

There may be disabilities, from eyesight to hearing to lack of a limb or tail, that may disqualify an individual based on some random attribute. Further, ambiguity in what may qualify under the class or kind of dog may exist, such as including or excluding wolves, coyotes, or hybrids.

Standards Wars

In my previous book, I detailed the conflict between standards practitioners (and users of standards) that sit in two different camps; those supporting multiple standards versus those advocating for a single standard across numerous domains and use cases. While I may have taken the examples of fasteners and dogs to an extreme, hopefully they provide a more accessible example of actual problems in creating and applying standards around data, and how solutions can be framed in either a one-for-everything versus one-per-use case issue.

Some conflicting standards efforts have resulted in real legal battles, such as in the cases of PVC versus metal pipe standards in the United States and Microsoft XML standards efforts in ISO. And the issue has not gone unnoticed by the standards organizations themselves.

In 2011, the American Nation Standards Institute (ANSI), with support from the National Institute on Standards and Technology (NIST), hosted a workshop entitled "Standards Wars: Myth of Realty? How the forces of competition, convergence and coordination impact standards development."[†] With close to 300 participants, the workshop aimed to discuss, among other things, "where conflict and duplication in standards development have been intentional in response to stakeholder needs, and unintentional due to lack of awareness of existing standardization efforts."[1]

In other words, it was to continue conversations alive in the standards community for decades regarding how, and even if, we should address conflict and duplication in standards. I identified two primary schools of thought: those who believe there are too many standards, which means there is no standard, and those who think multiple standards evolve to meet marketplace needs, showing demand for multiple standards, and creating a healthy and competitive environment.

A key point raised is that any policing or structuring in the standards system would necessarily hinder innovation. While there

---

[†] Accessed December 7, 2022, https://share.ansi.org/shared%20documents/Meetings%20and%20Events/Standards_Wars/SW%20Workshop%20Report.pdf

was wide acknowledgment of the benefit of consensus and working toward a single agreed standard solution, there was still recognition that "sometimes there is a compelling need for more than one standard, which translates into different or overlapping content."[2]

Alternatively, one panel did "recognize[d] that the existence of multiple standards efforts requires the expenditure of greater resources. While this may be an acceptable cost in some sectors, in others it can be a drain."[3]

In the end, the workshop did not mean to deliver a verdict but to start a dialogue on the issues surrounding multiple standards that appear to be conflicting, overlapping, or duplicative to some. The problem for many participants, but by no means held by all, seemed to rest in the understanding that there are sector-specific needs, competition needs, innovation-driven solutions that may directly mirror long-existing solutions, and instances where different stakeholders have related but different definitions of requirements that result in the need for more than one solution.

Unfortunately, this dialogue has not formally continued or grown to include the wider global standards community. The debate between some who believe in single standards versus those who advocate for multiple standards based on nuanced needs in the marketplace continues. Furthermore, as the pendulum swings and data become a more critically recognized need, those unfamiliar with the key issues look toward the simpler world—believing single standards can solve all problems. This results in further mixing the data code into a more formidable brick that is more difficult to crack.

More on Standards and Definitions

We can apply broad standards and terms to many different use cases, and CoPs will end up providing some functionality to diverse, conflicting implementations. Still, generic standards can work against the attempt to enable a single language across groups that interact. The alternative would be to create clear and uniquely defined standards specific to CoPs and their use cases. Yet, in this case, a highly specified term or definition may not transcend the divide between different CoPs in functionality and meaning.

One could attempt to force the application of a specific definition across this divide. Yet, multiple implications exist. Consider a single word with two different but related definitions, one for CoP "A" and a different meaning for CoP "B." Imagine the definition for CoP "A" is, through some standardization process, deemed the only proper definition and is expected to be used across both communities.

The result would be a solution that works for CoP A, but CoP B must adjust. CoP B, internal to its processes, definitions, and functions, will likely not incorporate the CoP A meaning, but it will sit outside the regime. The adjustment introduces multiple issues regarding quality and ongoing maintenance. The definition may become stale to CoP A. Over time, those involved with any negotiation with CoP A will move on, forget, or lose the context of any agreement. CoP B will also be evolving at the same time. So, any agreed adjustments or adoption by CoP B to accommodate are tactical and temporary.

The first practical implications also rest with any processes, procedures, technical infrastructure, and legal dependencies the change to the definition will have within CoP "B." The second practical implication is that the original definition still has meaning within CoP "B"; therefore, we need to invent a new or altered term to capture that essence of meaning to mitigate the impacts of the first implication.

We use definitions in two ways. In a general sense, it is to describe something. But, in most instances, we look to define something in a way that incorporates properties that relate to the purpose or function for which we need to use the term. This use drives the required data, how it is defined, how and where it is stored, and for what purpose or use.

To give a specific example for the CoP A versus B discussion, let's consider one general term. The term *trade* presents such a definition challenge. As a generic term, it could be accepted across financial services as it means exchanging some things of value between two or more parties.

However, this is likely insufficient for practical uses when used in practice. Governments may talk about trade deficits or surpluses, which are a wholly different sort of trade than a front office broker envisions when discussing a trade. While the contexts that separate these two definitions may be apparent to financial professionals, the difference in what a trade encompasses becomes more nuanced when trying to more precisely define what a trade is to an investment manager, a custodian, a beneficiary, a broker, or a regulator. The concept of trade changes through the operational lifecycle as activities move from one to the next.

A nonexhaustive list of examples of *trade:*

CoP	Trade meaning(s)
Front office	Can refer to an order from a customer or prime broker, an individual execution on an exchange at a specific price, or an averaged priced trade (multiple executions make up a larger trade to fill multiple orders). Trades on exchange will be directed to settle at the central counterparty but may be netted.
Investment manager	Front office order to broker (which can span multiple portfolios), block trade directed to the custodian (made up of individual trades across portfolios), a single trade within a single portfolio.
Middle office	Block trade to be confirmed, individual trades (either part of a block or one of their own) to be confirmed.
Back office (Custody/Investment manager)	Individual trade within a single account to be settled at central depository.
Back office (broker)	Individual trade to be settled at depository for a client. Also it could be netted settlements being settled within a central counterparty.

Furthermore, a broker may agree that most of the different types of transactions they deal in are all *trades* but then clarify them through attached terms like *exchange trade, client order, trade allocation, partial trade,* and so forth.

Most of this nuance would not be apparent or known to those without direct contact with the broker's front office. Custodians wouldn't be dealing with the individual exchange executions, only the final average price trade. So, they have no context to consider a definition different from their own. That final trade may be just a single allocation of a larger block trade that the custodian is not privy to because the manager has distributed accounts across multiple custodians. Yet, this fact makes no difference in the single custodian back office settlement CoP.

While one may argue that different terms do exist for other circumstances—for example, order, execution, trade, and so forth—it is typical for these terms to be used interchangeably within a singular CoP, and they either retain some nuanced difference in meaning or don't, depending on the circumstance and individuals involved.

Saussure discusses conceptual differences in words, such that "any conceptual difference perceived by the mind seeks to find expression through a distinct signifier, and two ideas that are no longer distinct in the mind tend to merge into the same signifier."[4] In the context of Communities of Practice, consider each CoP possesses its own *mind.* As such, if a CoP's uses do not have any meaningful impact on their processes or practices, they will not find differentiation between two similar terms that may have impactful meaning for some other CoP. In Eskimo-Aluet, multiple variations of the concept of *snow* convey a slightly different context of snow's existence and form. Someone who does not appreciate those differences (because they do not need to) will ask, "But they all mean snow, right?" This phenomenon, therefore, goes in both directions—one may not appreciate the different meanings that two or more similar utterances convey and thus use them interchangeably, or protest that since all the terms mean the same thing to them, they relate it only to an aggregated term of their choosing, ignoring the actual nuances.

A custodian may use the terms *order, execution,* and *trade* to refer to all the same thing—a transaction settling at the depository for their client's account (a delivery at DTCC is called a *Delivery Order*). Yet, these terms have vastly different interpretations within a broker's operations. At the same time, a broker may use the singular term *trade* to refer to the different contexts of *order*, *execution*, and *trade*—relying on the experience and knowledge of their co-workers to understand which concept they are referring to at any point and time.

The question then goes to how to structure the definition. Should the term be altered in such a way as to create distinction (e.g., exchange-based broker trade versus custody settlement trade) so that there are *unique* singular terms that then have a corresponding unique definition?

Or should the context be based on the definition and bound by the owner of the particular dictionary? In other words, the term *trade* is not clarified by other words attached. Still, instead, the fact that we define it within the front office, within the systems processing exchanged-based trades, gets captured in the attached metadata to provide its context within the CoP of the front office. The premise that the term *trade* in the database refers to an exchange execution is based on the facts of where that database resides, what processing system accesses it (or stores the data), the processes that result in that data exists, and the CoP that is performing the process and function (a little hint here—we are approaching the concepts that pertain to pragmatics now).

In the former solution, the expectation would have to be that all individuals and groups (CoPs) would need to adopt the precise terminology and for that terminology to persist everywhere. It would need to assume that no group would subsequently become lax about the burden of the clarifying term—that is no CoP would eventually begin to simplify their language and revert to only using the generic term *trade*, as within their community, *trade* already has a singular meaning. All other variants are other concepts unto themselves.

Next, consider two words or terms used for the exact definition in two other CoPs. In derivatives trading, the front office calls a particular number that they express as a percentage *price*; in the back office, they refer to this number as the *rate*. The reasoning is that before executing the trade, the percentage is constantly changing; this is the rate the trader will eventually agree upon and from which they calculate future values. Within the context of what they are doing—buying and selling financial instruments—this percentage number is a price. But for the back office, once the trade is executed and finalized, that percentage number stays the same—and is the rate used to calculate any number of things. Again, assume the term utilized by the front office CoP has forced adoption upon the back office CoP. From a language perspective, the most likely result is that in explaining what the term means, members of the back office language group will likely define it in context to their original term, not in the terms used by the front office language group, which can lead to confusion. The worst case scenario is that it conflicts with the term *price* in this or another related CoP but has a different meaning and increases errors.

CHAPTER 4

Applied Linguistics for the Layperson

As stated previously, we should acknowledge that multiple standards and financial languages are barriers to better transparency and regulation and impose actual economic costs. Perhaps counterintuitively, this is a stated property of language—that the nature of language to evolve and diversify harms the ability to communicate across the wider population.

However, the question remains unasked if enforcing a single, common, standardized financial language would provide better transparency and regulation or reduce costs (or at least not increase costs significantly).

The logic error here is assuming that because one existing problem is bad—multiple languages and standards—the direct opposite would be better by just being the opposite. Unfortunately, most problems are not this simple and binary. No existing study or research can prove that standardizing on a single language or standard solves the myriad of issues under multiple languages—especially without any negative impacts that may outweigh the original problems.

Consider the child who says "It hurts when I touch it." The response? "Then don't touch it." It is a simple and elegant solution, but it will not fix a cut or a broken bone that is the actual issue at hand. The important question to ask is why it hurts. Multiple languages cause a problem. Instead of *get rid of all languages*, perhaps we should understand why there are multiple languages.

The Problem With Language

Language sits at the core of our being as humans. Communication exists throughout all living things, and linguists and scientists have debated the existence of *nonhuman language*. Linguists from Chomsky, Wardhaugh, and Hockett have all proposed various theories, comparisons, and design features that all seek to clarify what qualifies as *language* and why it is a uniquely human creation. Language does not discount scientists who evaluate communication methods within and across species differently, and religions and philosophers who separately debate the concepts of language, awareness, and communication across a different perspective.

Without delving into the philosophy or science of the existence of language, we shall accept that language, as a construct, exists. But what defines a language? This simple question opens up a core reason for the field of linguistics existing in the first place—as there is still no agreement on what a *language* is. Introducing things like dialects and jargon adds further complications that, to the anthropologist linguist, have specific nuances that subjugate them to something lesser than the elevation of a *true* language.

Borrowing from John McWhorter's article in *The Atlantic,*[*] one may only think about human languages such as English, Spanish, German, Chinese, Japanese, and so on. Dialects come into play within these individual languages, exemplified by American English and British English as simple dialects of each other (not to mention English spoken by Americans in the Southern U.S. states or Queen's English versus Geordie[†]).

Mutual intelligibility can help distinguish a dialect from a language.[‡,§,¶] Most writings on the subject talk to "most linguists would agree" that mutual intelligibility is a measure that we can use to differentiate between a dialect and a language, at least by roughly estimating the level

---

[*] Accessed December 20, 2022, www.theatlantic.com/international/archive/2016/01/difference-between-language-dialect/424704/.

[†] There you go, Chris.

[‡] Accessed December 20, 2022, https://thelanguagedoctors.org/difference-between-dialect-and-language/.

[§] Accessed December 20, 2022, www.theatlantic.com/international/archive/2016/01/difference-between-language-dialect/424704/.

[¶] Accessed December 20, 2022, https://direct.mit.edu/coli/article/45/4/823/93361/How-to-Distinguish-Languages-and-Dialects.

at which two different forms of speech can be understood by speakers of two different dialects or languages.

For a linguist researching or tracing the evolution and classification of languages, the differences or similarities between languages, and how to link and tie them together are important. It allows for the lineage creation and traceability of changes based on factors like culture, migrations, geography, and so on.

However, in the day-to-day practice of communicating, mutual intelligibility does little to prevent language barriers that require conversational repair. For example, that previous sentence should (hopefully) make perfect sense to a linguist. However, for someone who is not versed in the jargon of linguistics, one likely would need to reread that first sentence and infer the meaning to something more like just because two people speak the same parent language, differences in the meaning of words based on a different dialect they speak will cause misunderstandings, that they will then have to ask the other speaker *what do you mean?*

I've used the simple example of the word *jumper*, which can mean various things based on dialect. An American speaker will not immediately understand that a British speaker means *sweater* in the utterance "I had to grab my jumper because it was cold." Either the American speaker will ask what a *jumper* is, or if they are from the mid-west, they may think that it was so cold the car battery died and they needed jumper cables to start their car!

Of course, an American and a British speaker can likely have an easier conversation than between someone who only speaks English and someone who only speaks Japanese. But for our purposes, in applying linguistic concepts within data, we should recognize the potential for errors in communicating and understanding to exist regardless of whether two things have different languages, dialects, or jargon.

There remains debate on determining what qualifies as a *language* and what relegates to the lower linguistic status of *dialect*, and further, *jargon*. There is a statement, attributed to sociolinguist Max Weinreich recounting a discussion with a Bronx high school teacher who quipped that the difference between language and dialect is that "a language is a dialect with an army and a navy."[**] This statement means that the difference between a language and a dialect is arbitrary and typically framed by those with more political or social power.

Does it have any relevant value if we call something a language or dialect? A Spanish speaker has some mutual intelligibility with a Portuguese speaker and even an Italian speaker. Yet, they classify as different languages. Scottish Standard English[††] is, in linguistic studies, considered an English dialect, yet it is arguably less mutually intelligible, as are some Swedish dialects. Earlier, I mentioned jargon, which is essentially specialized terminology associated with a specific profession, field, or activity as opposed to language and dialect. Jargon is sometimes called *slang* (with similar arguments about differentiating the two, as are those applied to language versus dialect). Slang, however, is more culturally generational, can be regional, and isn't linked to a profession or field of study like jargon. Generally, jargon (as opposed to a language) is more relatable to specific practices or activities with specialized terms and meanings. The words in this specialized vocabulary either carry different meanings than when used outside of this specific practice/activity or are invented and unintelligible to those outside of the specific practice/activity.

For example, if I were to talk about *weeding*, the general person would likely assume I was talking about gardening and getting rid of weeds. However, a librarian will probably consider removing books and other materials from a collection. There's a significant amount of business jargon such that if you are trying to move the needle, you may need to streamline and forget those out of the loop to create a win-win situation and shift the paradigm. While a jumble of nonsense buzzwords, there is utility in them. This jargon assists in conveying certain specialized meanings quickly to those "in the know," enabling better communication between participants. Of course, the downside is that anyone not 'in the know' has much more difficulty interacting and understanding.

[**] Accessed July 19, 2023, https://en.wikipedia.org/wiki/A_language_is_a_dialect_with_an_army_and_navy.

[††] Noting this is different than Scottish, which is a Germanic language in its own right.

Linguistics Versus Applied Linguistics

So, the chapter is called "Applied Linguistics for the Layperson." There is a difference between linguistics and applied linguistics, which we should explain. Linguistics is more about studying language—its creation, evolution, change, and usage. Much more scientific, linguistics dives into questions between dialect and language, how to classify languages, anthropology, and deep underlying reasons for change.

In contrast, applied linguistics aims to solve real-world problems using the various insights and knowledge gained through an understanding of linguistics. It is more about issues like sociolinguistic questions that revolve around language differences and conflicts, and how to use linguistic techniques to solve or better understand those issues.

Of course, that division is broad and subject to interpretation, as with all things in language. For example, some linguists will say that applied linguistics and sociolinguistics are different fields. And some may scoff at applied linguistics as being wholly unscientific and subjective. In any case, looking at data as language gives us a chance to step back and consider all that these disciplines have to teach us.

So, suppose we remove the distinction a linguist may place between a *language* and a *dialect*. In that case, we can simplify and say that dialects are unique languages closely related to other languages, usually spoken by people in geographical proximity. This removal leaves other distinctions like jargon, which we discussed above, and a new one, creole.

Creole is the mixing of different languages that morphs into a new language. Starting as a *pidgin* (a simplified language to enable two different language groups to communicate), creole languages develop as adults teach their children, and this new form becomes their primary language. Those in the Southeast of the United States should be familiar with the Louisiana Creole (*cajun*) language, one well-known example. Cajun creole resulted from a mixing of French colonizers in the New Orleans area, French-speaking Canadians who migrated in the 18th century from the Acadia region (shortened to *Cajuns*), enslaved Africans from the Senegambia region, and the original Native American inhabitants.[‡‡] Creole languages are useful in a community where the population overlaps two or more language geographies, and the local language evolves as a merger of two or more languages.

As defined above, jargon tends to be expressions specific to a particular discipline or field. Jargon's usefulness is its ability to convey information between people in the same specialized area quickly. The argument against jargon is that it is a significant barrier to understanding for anyone who does not belong to or has expertise in that specialized field.

Jargon appears in many varied places. Most sports have their jargon, for example. A *hole* in baseball usually refers to the space between the third baseman and the shortstop. A *pitch* in football (known to Americans as soccer) is the field on which we play the game, not someone throwing a ball to the batter. Also, in football, there are tactics like *route one* (a direct playing style) or descriptive phrases like *hospital ball*[§§] (a bad pass of the ball to a teammate that forces them into a situation where they could very likely get hurt). In American football, you have a *strong side* (usually the side of the field with the most players lined up for a play, but not always[¶¶]) and a *weak side*. In all these cases, Jargon allows those who are *in the know* and either play or follow a certain sport to convey concepts that otherwise require more explanation or description quickly. At the same time, the terms in use have little to no meaning (or completely different meanings) to outsiders. So, after that long walk, we have identified one of the problems with language: defining and identifying what language is!

[‡‡] Accessed July 21, 2023, https://en.wikipedia.org/wiki/Louisiana_Creole#:~:text=Louisiana%20Creole%20is%20a%20French,well%20as%20Cajun%20and%20Creole.
[§§] In Rugby football, known as a hospital pass.
[¶¶] When a single tight end is used, the strong side is the side they are on, regardless of number of offensive players.

Languages, Languages, Everywhere!

Up to this point, we have mainly discussed language in the context of the human languages everyone is familiar with. However, this is only one way to view language. Most of us would not recognize that we encounter dozens of what could be classified as languages daily.

When you have car trouble and bring it to a mechanic, they tell you what is wrong. Manifolds, alternators, camshafts, pistons ... we may have learned these words over the years. Still, many generally don't know what they are, why they are important, and what possibly has gone wrong with them. All we know is that the expert mechanic seems to know what they are talking about, and yes, please, fix that.

This experience repeats across different industries. It is also one reason I rarely go to coffee shops. I cannot understand their lexicon and feel like a tourist out of sorts, even thinking of ordering anything other than a medium coffee. Sorry, order me a medium *Americano*. I have no idea what a half-caf, venti, double latte Caramello is. Don't get me started on macchiato.

However, sticking with the theme of financial services, I brought forward the argument in the previous book that financial services operate as a larger social system with multiple parts, each of which has its distinct language (Communities of Practice).

For those outside of financial services, the terms and language used can sound as foreign as the language used by the car mechanic. Rates, ratios, call dates, inverted curve ... there is a bit of faith most people put in their banker when discussing mortgages and loans, or the relative benefits of exchange-traded funds (ETFs) over single stocks when deciding on investments with their financial adviser.

We should be ignoring traditional human language for this discussion—even as these industry-based languages all exist within a single *human* language like English[***] they are not intelligible to everyone who speaks English. As the saying goes, once you venture

---

[***] I'm going to default to English here because I am not human language bilingual.

into a specialized industry without expertise or knowledge, it is "All Greek to me."[†††, ‡‡‡]

In the previous section, as a convenience, we dispensed with the differentiation between language and dialect, jargon and creole. So this leaves us with the question of what differentiates languages. When we look at this world of specialized *practice* or *domain* language, how exactly do we separate them? We can pursue two primary pathways— one scientific and mathematical, and the other more subjective.

Mathematically, we could examine the normal distribution of speech variation between two selected dictionaries and devise a measure that says anything over the "x" percentage of differentiation would be considered a candidate for being a distinct language.

Subjectively, it could be a matter of looking at culture, identifying some other sociological measurements, looking at what may be a social system, and then the communities that operate within it to make it function. Mutual intelligibility also comes into play.

I previously leveraged the work of Wenger-Trayner and their work around CoP.[§§§] Specifically,

> Communities of practice are groups of people who share a
> concern or a passion for something they do and learn how to
> do it better as they interact regularly.[¶¶¶]

[†††,] So, I did present at a Greek language financial services data conference hosted by Bourissa. I presented in English, and I suspect when translated to Greek, it was unintelligible to anyone not involved in financial services data, even if they spoke Greek.

[‡‡‡] As an aside, there are some sources that assign this expression to scribes in Medieval or even Roman times that would write Graecum est, non legitur or Graecum est, non potest legi (It is Greek; it cannot be read), at sections they could not translate. However, there is firm proof of it being used by Shakespeare in 1599, in The Tragedy of Julius Caesar. Casca says "it was Greek to me" about a speech he found unintelligible. To complete this aside, Baltic countries tend to use Spanish as the unintelligible language in the idiom instead of Greek, and Greeks and many others refer to Chinese.

[§§§] Accessed December 21, 2022, www.wenger-trayner.com/introduction-to-communities-of-practice/.

[¶¶¶] Ibid.

As discussed previously, identifying the domain, community, and practice are keys to bounding this collection of linked individuals who, through their shared activities and function, developed a shared "repertoire of resources," specializing and, through this, creating their language, which is specific to their community.

CoPs are not, on the whole, neat, self-contained isolated systems. As parts of social systems, they interact with other communities and systems in the wider human society. One could draw broad brush-strokes in defining a community of practice, but we must also consider what defines a social system. Wenger-Trayner notes "A community of practice itself can be viewed as a simple social system. And a complex social system can be viewed as constituted by interrelated communities of practice."[1]

That is to say, a CoP should take a constitutional form as simple as possible. As a nonexpert, nonmember of a particular social system, we will tend to erringly view some social system as a simple CoP unto itself. We use broad domain labels like *retail, manufacturing, medical,* and *financial services* and view them as homogeneous communities, which then encourages us to assume these systems share a single language.

Yet, as I've explored, something like *financial services* is not a single community but an extensive social system of many different CoPs that overlap and interact. Each of the individual CoPs has special- ized, and in that specialization, language evolves and becomes more specific and unique to each community. As this coincides throughout all the different CoPs within the broader social system, divergence in language (and data) between communities increases—even connected communities. Further, new communities emerge, further fragmenting the language landscape.

Even when you identify a seemingly homogeneous community, a closer look may reveal language and data differences that we must consider. So, simply stating that there is a single *financial language* that we can use ignores the vast diversity within financial services. The similarities are easy to gather and use as *proof* that all financial services have a common foundation and must speak the same language. While

all romance languages have a common Latin base, we would not claim
that French and Italian are the same.

For example, one could point to global accounting rules as the
basis for a single financial language. Yet, there are different rules
there, as well—FASB[****] and IFRS.[††††] Further, not all financial
language speaks to accounting—you can study microeconomics, which
is distinctly different from macroeconomics. Again, all the information
is related but distinctly different, meant for different purposes and
to examine different things. Accounting data is not used in trading,
though we may derive accounting data from trading activity, derive
being the key term, as we cannot use the exact data.

The same is valid for reporting regimes, for example, MiFID[‡‡‡‡]
and MiFIR.[§§§§] Front-office transaction reporting has a different
purpose than posttrade regulatory reporting. So, for these different
reporting regimes, attempting to use the executions reported of trade
surveillance (more of a MiFID) focus for posttrade (more of a MiFIR
focus) does not make sense. Prices mean different things, come from
different sources, and do not correlate for many reasons.

Some Applied Linguistics Tools

In the first book, I introduced five aspects that surround language:

- Communities of Practice
- Language constantly evolves
- There is no right or wrong language
- Language exists in a multitude of forms
- Language is a social construct

These aspects are, admittedly, a subjectively cobbled-together list of
what I felt were the most applicable properties for creating a foundation
for the discussion in that book. I also included a brief on Langefors'
study of infological models and the concepts of accommodation and

---

[****] Financial Accounting Standards Board.
[††††] International Financial Reporting Standards.
[‡‡‡‡] Markets in Financial Instruments Directive.
[§§§§] Markets in Financial Instruments Regulation.

repair (which I incorrectly referred to *repair* as *fixing* throughout the first book).⁵⁵⁵⁵

As a refresher, I'll start with language evolution. Language is constantly evolving. Language does not remain static, as new words come into being that better reflect the current culture or occurrences in a society. By the same method, existing words may change in meaning over time or as one language group drifts apart due to various factors, not limited to cultural, geography, or societal influences. Further, as two (or more) different speech groups encounter and interact more or less, their languages will change and evolve.

One of the underlying factors for this evolution is the existence of language as a social construct. What this means is that language does not exist in itself. A society creates it as a means of enabling communication among the members of that community. Some would say that language is a cognitive construction for social needs, but this is splitting hairs for our purposes. It is enough to acknowledge that language is created, through some human process, for an end social means. The essential thing to realize is that language evolves and diversifies because it simultaneously makes it easier and more efficient for a single speech community to communicate among its members.

The Sommelier

I once had the lucky opportunity to attend a virtual wine tasting hosted by a sommelier during the 2020 pandemic. I have been chastised throughout my years, for erring in which glass I should use for this or that particular variety of wine. So, with a professional there, I asked, "What is the right glass to use with each type of wine?"

The sommelier noted that this was a question that he fielded very often. In response, he picked up one of the bottles we were sampling and took a drink right from the bottle! Putting it down, he noted, "What vessel you use to convey your wine to your mouth is

---

⁵⁵⁵⁵ Doubtful I will forgive myself for that mistake, though philosophically, I could defend myself with the rule that there is no right or wrong language.

important only in that it functions properly in conveying your wine into your mouth effectively."

He then explained that the type of vessel used for a particular wine, or even a wine pairing, is more a function of people wishing to impose some view of sophistication or special knowledge. You don't have to have red wine with beef or only drink white wine from a special "white wine glass." The only right or wrong is if you can drink the wine, which tastes good with your meal. The "you need to use this glass for this wine" rigor is the province of people who feel better looking down on others who don't know what they know.

So, this social construct observation ties in with language evolution, as society changing and evolving should typically also have an evolution of language within that society. Related to this is the existence of language in a multitude of forms. A single word's meaning may differ depending on the use and context of that word—witness that there are multiple meanings for the deceptively simple word *lead* —and there also may be many different words that have the same meaning. The form language takes is not dependent upon what it conceptually describes, but the meaning is assigned to the language by the speech community.

If a speech community assigns language, the argument concerns *right* versus *wrong* language. As with my experience with the sommelier, evaluating a specific use of language as right or wrong is more of a political domain than linguistics. Like the wine vessel, the critical thing to consider is if the language conveys the meaning it needs. The unfortunate thing here, especially in data management, is that those viewing the *rightness* or *wrongness* of any data or language are not typically primary members of the speech community they are evaluating. Further, those considering meaning and language may have a vested interest in preserving the *rightness* of their language in the face of others using a *wrong* language.

In human language, I have in the past pointed to the Hamburg Empire's restrictions on local languages, the conflict between those wishing to preserve Shakespearian English against the tide of backward

American English (as best told by Mencken), or the pushing of legislation in various U.S. states and Congress to enforce English-speaking requirements over enabling non-English speaking immigrant groups, most notably Spanish speakers.[2]

Tying together a multitude of forms (and the *Use Theory of Meaning*), with evolution and the social construct of language, the existence of power and politics around language should not be a great surprise. As such, I will continue to bring in the problem of the tendency of groups to enforce the classification of data definitions and language of other groups as right or wrong, with the explicit goal of attempting to mitigate this influence.

We arrive at my first original aspect—the Community of Practice. The CoP is a form of a speech community, defined through a social structure where language has evolved via specialization to allow that community to come together around a mutual engagement in some joint endeavor. This community is not some ad hoc group but one that has defined social culture and norms. When two or more CoP come into a linguistic conflict, our data management problems regarding right or wrong language become apparent.

Written and Stored Data (Language) and Its Complications

As I will delve further into how to use applied linguistics to address foundational data organization and understanding, it would help to give a more detailed examination of language and its properties. Hopefully, a more encompassing base in applied linguistics, at least from my layperson's perspective, will let the reader begin to see this different perspective and how other speech groups influence data.

In *Mapping Applied Linguistics*, the first subchapter is entitled, "Why do we use different languages?" In short, the authors argue that there is a significant social aspect to language diversity and a biological one. A child's language is never a perfect copy of their parents for many reasons—one is that language is learned and acquired, and each individual will receive language from multiple sources. Language "has evolved not just to serve the individual user, but also to serve the group."[3]

The concept that language serves the group's needs is key to understanding how social systems, like financial services, function and use distinct and different language groups. There is no *better language*—one community's language is not somehow superior or better than another. However, the idea that some groups don't use their language correctly is a persistent accusation throughout history. "Many such beliefs arise naturally because of mistrust of 'The Other', but in large part language judgements follow the notion of a 'standard' form of the language against which all other varieties can be measured—and found wanting."[4]

This accusation is a trap that data and language fall into—many times since they are expressions of language, not spoken language. To record data (language), one must write it down in some fashion. Language has only been widely accessible in written form for a few hundred years. Even going back to early Greek and Chinese civilizations, written language was the purview of the elite—a closed and small community among themselves. While written and stored data (language) has its benefits in preservation and ability to transmit to significantly more people than spoken speech in more methods and mediums, it is subject to many failings. Stored data is influenced by those that keep it—intentionally or unintentionally—and therefore carries bias in its meaning, even apart from the social power and control concerns noted above. Stored data can also be lost, damaged, or miscopied or society can lose the ability to access (read) the information stored. If it were not for the multilingual Rosetta Stone, we would still be unable to read Ancient Egyptian hieroglyphs.

The simple ability to store or record data (language) falsely leads one to believe we can fully standardize it into a single form and meaning. There is an inherent catch-22 in stored and written data and language. We know that a core property of language is to continuously evolve and evolve within speech communities, diverging from each other over time. Even within a single community, speech may split and drift apart. But to record data and language, one needs to create a single static (e.g., standard), unchanging representation of the language at a particular point in time.

An argument could be that written and stored language has mainly remained intelligible while language evolves. And because of this, we shouldn't be concerned about language drift regarding stored and written data. But the counterargument would appear more substantial. While we may prove written and stored language to be largely intelligible over time, it also requires more effort at interpretation and deciphering—even for native speakers. Our understanding of the U.S. Constitution over time has not been one that has created more clarity and certainty but more diverse interpretations and less certainty of meaning. Reading Shakespeare or even the more modern Keats is no simple task for modern English speakers. Yet, language can also make rapid, sudden changes in meaning, and its stored representation will no longer match the new definition. Further, newly stored data will be held in the new meaning, creating a schism between existing and newly stored data.

This language variety conflicts heavily with the individual's (and data manager's) notion that a single standard version of language exists, typically centered on and around their native language or subject matter expertise. Therefore, we ignore it in the data analysis and creation of data storage, and it is more damaging in its extraction, transformation, and ingest elsewhere.

Ignoring Discourse Analysis at Your Peril

Discourse, very basically, is conversation. It is the transfer of information via language between two entities (people, parties, or, however, you wish to term them). The applied linguist's goal in analyzing discourse is to find "how does the study of discourse illuminate the cultural and social processes that can lead to language-related problems, and solutions, for our clients?"[5] So, for a data manager, why does this even matter? We aren't discussing cultural or social processes in communicating data across the financial system, right?

OK, that was an unfair and loaded question. Of course, we are talking about culture and social processes. While we don't inherently think of them as such, the methods and functions of our various CoPs are instances or expressions of a sort of underlying cultural and social existence within the overall social system of financial services (or whichever industry you operate in). Data managers do not store data for the simple act of recording but to communicate that data to others to satisfy some function or process that supports a CoP's overall reason for being.

This data will be part of a discourse between those who created it and those who eventually use it. There are many approaches to discourse analysis which are relevant for different purposes and scenarios. I will not cover most linguistic and social discourse analysis approaches. There is too much detail, and my goal is foundational. For example, corpus linguistics would likely find relevance among data managers dealing with problems surrounding data lakes or other large data stores that are of a similar variety—that is, from a more homogenous population that aligns with a single Community of Practice (remembering that CoPs exist in a matrix such that this may span horizontally or vertically across multiple other CoPs—the key point is that the primary language is of that one CoP as opposed to any of the other slices).

But for our purposes, looking at contrasting CoPs, *Speech Act Theory* holds more relevance as "part of the wider discipline of pragmatics. The work of philosopher J.L. Austin provided pragmatics with a theoretical framework for understanding the relationship between speaker, hearer, utterance and context (Austin, 1975)."[6] This work provides the basis for the concept of a speech act, which involves not just the basic semantics of the data nor the context it exists in, but the entire ecosystem around the *act* of the data we communicate. That is the hearer—whoever is receiving and interpreting the data, what community in which they exist, and the context of not just the intended meaning of the data, but under the conditions of its use, and where at that moment, as well as prior use and experiences.

Chief data officers typically work at an enterprise more holistically, with the need to have a perspective across an entire firm. As we've explored, these organizations will have multiple CoPs with different languages to fight against any monolithic data definitions (unless their data definitions happen to be the monolithic language, of course!). And my more recent experiences in forums and industry groups have not changed much in the past 5 or even 10 years—the biggest struggle is with disparate datasets, different definitions, and interoperability between functional areas and "breaking down silos."

In linguistic terms, it is the discourse between heterogeneous language groups that chief data officers and data managers struggle with the most. In partnership with speech acts, interactional sociolinguistics may also be an area of interest. Given the different perspectives of interacting CoPs, interactional sociolinguistics would be a more cultural-focused program around context-bound interpretation and discovering reasons for misinterpretation between functional areas identified as separate CoPs that must interact but typically clash in communication. The interaction would naturally also bring in concepts of intercultural communication within discourse analysis.

But how does this help a data manager? Approaches today are not working. They run the gamut, from strict centralist approaches, where we expect everyone to conform to a single organization-wide vocabulary, to federated, where every functional area manages their data according to some central guiding principles. This approach maps from these federated definitions to a central "single source of truth" to enable cross-organizational interoperability. In none of these approaches are common language groups formally defined or discovered. Shared processes are still troubled by multiple definitions and meanings, and who owns the data steward role drives what gets recorded. Further, who the data steward represents is not defined formally compared to other data stewards and the overall organization.

However, even a rudimentary foray into discourse analysis, after formally defining language groups around their CoP, could significantly enhance how a data manager views and approaches their data architecture. A technology-agnostic process allows a data manager to see how and where language differs across their organization and where language problems exist.

Repair and Accommodation

One of the hallmarks of human spoken communication is the ability to resolve communication problems due to language differences. The resolution is through two functions: repair and accommodation. I briefly introduced these topics and covered them in the first book. However, it is important to provide a review as a critical part of the communication landscape.

Repair in discourse is when we discover an error in understanding between speaker and hearer, and then further communication is performed to resolve that error.

Repair can occur between two members of the same language. However, the more interesting aspect of dealing with multiple CoPs is the repair between two participants from different language groups. Four general types of repair[7] are as follows:

- Self-initiated, self-repair: the speaker realizes there is a miscommunication and acts to resolve it.
- Other-initiated, self-repair: the listener indicates a miscommunication, and the speaker makes an effort to clarify and resolve it.
- Self-initiated, other repair: the speaker attempts to have the listener repair the miscommunication, such as by prompting the listener to provide the right word to use.
- Other-initiated, other-repair; the listener, effectively, corrects the speaker.

In contrast, accommodation looks to avoid the need for repair by one, or both, of the participants making changes in their language to align with the language of the other participant.

Language repair may seem trivial, as we do it through the normal course of conversation. Conversation, generally, is *turn-based*—so one participant speaks, the other listens, and then the roles may reverse. It is during these turns that miscommunications can be found and resolved.

So, how is this relevant to data managers? In thinking about how we end up with our data dictionaries and business requirement documents, we usually accomplish the repair function during the requirements gathering phase and testing. After implementation, no dynamic, turn-based, automated repair occurs within the system, database, or dictionary. Attempts at repair may occur after deploying a system or data dictionary, and users point out what they consider to be errors or things that are unclear or do not make sense. But in many cases, repairs expect users to adopt any new terminology or definitions or at least learn how to translate for themselves on the fly.

Many could point to communication protocol standards as addressing and solving for the lack of an ability to perform discourse repair in fields like financial services that require different CoPs to exchange information. FIX, ISO20022, ISO15022, and FpML are all standards that establish data fields and definitions to enable the exchange of information for everything from trading to settlement.

However, for practitioners in the standards space who work on developing and maintaining these standards, significant work goes on to enable a single message to be created by one CoP and then processed and understood correctly by another CoP. Committees work together, with representatives from the different CoPs, to analyze fields, agree on definitions, and create volumes of documentation on market practices and usage rules. Many of these, such as the global market practices created through ISITC NA,[*****] exist outside the actual standard documentation and are typically longer and more detailed than the standard itself. Many are volunteer-led organizations, such as the Securities Market Practice Group (SMPG) and the Payments Market Practice Group (PMPG), where members spend extra, unpaid time with their employer's tacit support. Further, these efforts are continuous and under constant revision and evolution. We can classify this activity as a way to try and resolve discourse problems in light of an inability to perform *live* repair or accommodation during actual communication.

We should recognize that data communication standards do not appear to remove ambiguity, enable error-free communication, or unify different CoP languages. Significant effort remains in separate activities to perform repair and accommodation as independent processes.

[*****] ISITC NA is an international market practice industry association based in the United States (ISITC.org).

The 2008 Financial Crisis

The 2008 crash and Lehman debacle most exemplify the economic cost argument of language divergence. This event highlighted the lack of transparency caused by different financial languages and the difficulty in tracing what happened, why, and how to unravel it. Multiple papers and analyses have shown how this fragmentation contributed to the 2008 crash. "Creating a Linchpin for Financial Data: The Need for a Legal Entity Identifier"[8] examines how the fragmented methodologies and definitions used for identifying legal entities contributed to the inability to judge risk exposure and consistently identify legal entities, particularly referencing the complex Lehman Brothers' corporate structures.

The "Financial Crisis Inquiry Report"[†††††] points to "the corrosion of mortgage-lending standards," lack of understanding of various financial products, and lack of transparency generally as contributing factors to the credit crisis of 2008. Essentially, data about mortgage assets and securitized products was either incorrect, missing, or misinterpreted (purposefully or unknowingly), contributing to further dirtying of what was incorrectly assumed to be reliable data.

The interesting thing about many of these examinations is that they assume an underlying consistency and shared knowledge across the entire financial system, as well as by those *outside* the financial system. That is, it assumes all those inside the financial system understand each other and are either purposely fraudulent or naively ignorant to the facts as we know them today, such as repackaging bad mortgages as securitized investment vehicles with high ratings they do not deserve. At the same time, the same examinations indicate that the end investors were wholly duped and ignorant of the existing risks because they were given intentionally false information or insufficient transparency to research and make determinations independently.

Indeed, the Commission Report states, "Those conditions created increased risks, which should have been recognized by market participants, policy makers, and regulators."[‡‡‡‡‡] (p. 26). This report rests upon

---

[†††††]www.govinfo.gov/content/pkg/GPO-FCIC/pdf/GPO-FCIC.pdf.
[‡‡‡‡‡]Ibid.

an assumption that every group performing specific functions shared the same understanding, data definitions, and purpose—from mortgage originators in the local retail market to institutional traders globally. It may be a leap to state that these groups should have recognized all the issues.

The resulting analysis states that it was either that the different participants did not understand the data they had—due to the complexity of new types of financing and rapid market changes—or they ignored the information and "chose poorly"[§§§§§] (p. 7). The assumption is that this points to a conclusion that data standardization across all facets of the industry would be the right solution. Yet, it ignores its conclusion in the problem statement. Specifically, each group in the chain of events did not understand the groups they interacted with or the exposure to the overall social system. It is questionable, then, that simply standardizing data would convey the experience and knowledge to understand that data, regardless of where in the system you are located.

Knowing a word's definition, even given an example, does not mean that you have the context or experience to understand it. Suppose one knows that a fixed income dirty price curve is a set of lines based on interest payments made toward maturity. In that case, that doesn't give you any insight into whether that is a good or bad investment, safe or risky, or how payments happen throughout the bond's life. As such, it asks if we require more information versus ensuring people receiving or reviewing data are better educated in what that data means, especially from communities that speak different languages.

There was a significant breakdown within the financial system. And some undoubtedly unscrupulous actors took advantage of systemic issues to benefit themselves. What is less certain is if the financial system and all the players actively worked together to fleece the general population. Indeed, a break in communication and understanding was at play. As a core issue, lowering mortgage lending standards introduced new factors we did not account for, even if the enablement of higher homeownership was a positively desired outcome. However, the charge that market participants (and policy makers and regulators) should have

---

[§§§§§] Ibid.

recognized is the increased risks assume a robust working communication network that transcended CoP language differences, not to mention precise knowledge that spans beyond macro and microeconomics and into the day-to-day functional operational activities that occur across a spectrum of interconnected communities. There seemed to be a working assumption that existing checks and balances would ensure no problems would arise, even though those checks and balances changed.

If we look at the crisis through the lens of applied linguistics, we may gain a different understanding of what happened. It doesn't absolve any actors, but it may help explain the disconnect between what many say was plain to see and the seemingly blind decisions made.

CHAPTER 5

Semantics Is Just Semantics

Ask almost any data practitioner, and you will hear that semantics are the key to solving any data riddle. Most will then pause and add, well, semantics and context. Some may also add tables to created classes or types to identify and merge terms where there may be semantic differences we don't want and cobble them together. So, is semantics the be-all-end-all answer or not?

There is simultaneously a call for capturing all different definitions for terms and simultaneously for creating a common vocabulary. The usual argument is first to capture all definitions and their sources. Then, populate these into a new *common data dictionary* for an entire enterprise. The next step is to go through similar terms with different definitions, especially where sources interact, and go through a consensus process to harmonize* those terms and adopt an agreed definition so that Group A's definition of *customer* is the same as Group B's definition of *customer*.

There is an irony in this—acknowledging many different ways people view and define things, yet expecting them to all agree on a single method.

Data managers have rallied around that a *concept* is important, not the words used to describe that *concept* and its meaning, as it aligns with the linguistic premise of arbitrariness—the absence of connection between a word's meaning and its sound or form (Saussure). We explored this in the previous section regarding the word *dog*.

Semantically, the term we assign to any particular concept shouldn't matter. So, by focusing purely on concepts within financial services data, the argument follows that a standard dictionary of common *concepts* can

---

* "Harmonize" usually ends up actually mean "pick one definition and make everyone use it." Usually, this is the definition that belongs to the strong political group.

be created, and then the arbitrary terms used to identify those concepts can be cataloged by data source and resolved cross-enterprise.

For example, how should a data manager capture and quantify the financial instrument known as a bond? Conceptually, it is a financial product that some entity has promised to pay back a certain amount of money, along with an additional cash flow. However, this does not tell the data manager what properties are important to capture. Or that there are also bonds that do not have a cash flow. The concept is important, but it doesn't help to communicate whatever is considered the *important* information. And there needs to be an acknowledgment that what is deemed *important* will differ based on who is asking and who is telling.

We further enforce this example by assuming that all financial concepts are math-based and, therefore, we can express them as singular concepts. Many data folks will point out that all financial data is simply accounting information, and we can reduce it to purely mathematical rules. However, there is a recognition that *context* matters.

The trouble in this effort is that concepts must use words to describe them. And those words are contextually impacted regarding the semantic interpretation any one CoP may bring. This effort is not a useless or impossible exercise. But it can become recursive.

Context

Context. What is context? In data management, we throw it about almost as much as the term semantics. But what do we mean? Is it the process being performed where we use the data? Is it the domain where we use the term versus another domain? How is *context* even bound or defined?

Ostensibly, context is being used as a variable to differentiate different semantic meanings for the same *term*. However, there is no unified view on how context is defined by data professionals in any particular industry, as we even use context to disambiguate similar concepts. This lack of unification points to data managers' difficulties in resolving data definitions, especially when conflicts arise between seemingly similar communities of practice.

Perhaps asking "What causes context?" would be one starting point before classifying two semantic meanings using context. Context is not a quantitative concept—it is the result or outcome of other underlying forces, so it becomes problematic to use it in a vacuum to differentiate semantic meaning.

There are multiple forms of context. Linguistic context involves what has been said before in a conversation or the other words included in any utterance or statement. Meanwhile, social context surrounds the community, communities, or social system(s) involved in the conversation. Epistemic context looks at what is known by both the speaker and hearer. Physical context involves the time and place of any utterance. Physical context could be viewed as situational context, though situational context may be more expansive and involve social and epistemic elements, among others.

The form of context is one important factor, but so is the goal of context.

Knowing the goal of a context permits an appropriate inter-pretation of a text. General objective contexts appear as true statements, such as scientific facts. They are usually found in documents such as scientific papers and news articles. Subjec-tive contexts include feelings, beliefs, and opinions. Probabil-ity contexts are comprehended in human inference and as a consequence of human languages. Time and space contexts occur in human reasoning and language. Domain contexts concern restrictions regarding the domain of applicability of a statement. Necessity contexts specify necessary conditions for something to happen, for example, the verb "must." Planning contexts involve information about someone's plans or wishes. When several contexts of different types overlap or coincide, a richness in information rather than conflict is achieved (Fortu and Moldovan 2005, pp. 171–173).[1]

Effective communication relies on understanding of context, at the point of communication. "Successful communication is assured when the hearer properly interprets two contexts: the discourse context, that is, the information contained in the words, and the physical social context, that is, the hearer's knowledge of the speaker, environment, and circumstances (Kreidler 1998, p. 23)."[2] Nouraldeen states this more simply—"Meaning and context are interrelated in a variety of situations. Successful communication cannot be achieved without the integration of meaning and context."[3]

Therefore, data, being stored meaningfully, needs to be interpreted in context. However, storing data with context is not a common practice (especially the qualities that surround and result in that context). Perhaps some metadata surrounds datasets, but typically, we exclude context because of the assumption the Community of Practice knows the context and will later be using the data. This interpretation of context refers to both the form of context and the goal of context. The goal of context within a domain is informed and inferred heavily by the CoP itself, as well as the goals and processes of a CoP. But just knowing what CoP may have stored any bit of data gives no context or knowledge insight into those goals and processes, which have the most significant influence on underlying and intended meaning.

Context, then, provides a view of the environment of an utterance to provide insight into additional or different meanings than a purely semantic reading may provide. Context is a set of factors that may come in various forms, but are generally not overly subjective, and are directly related to understanding and comprehending the intended meaning.

Context is different from perspective and bias. Bias we will discuss next, in greater detail. Meanwhile, using perspective as a transition to bias from context is interesting. Perspective involves shifting a frame of reference, or opinion, on how to interpret something. So, how is this different from context?

Context doesn't change. You may find more contextual clues or factors, but they were always there. However, perspective takes what we say in all its context and introduces another comparing factor. For example, two people may be friends, and one says, "You can be such a jerk sometimes." Now, in the context of them being friends, regardless of how one person makes the utterance—whether jokingly or seemingly meaning it, the two participants involved understand the context is not an accusation or implied to be an admonishment.

Now, imagine the conversation in a group setting, and one of the people present does not know the speaker. Even knowing the context, their perspective may be that it is a hurtful thing to say, especially if they are particularly close to the accused person. The misunderstanding must be resolved, not because of lack of context, but because of perspective.

While not precisely the same, perspective and bias are closely linked, just as context and perspective are somewhat linked.

Indirect, Direct, and Reported Speech

There are many nuances around what is considered reported speech. We can take the most general and encompassing view that reported speech is anything we didn't say ourselves. If we are repeating what someone else said, it is reported speech. If we write down what we said and give it to someone to read later, it is reported speech.

Reported speech can be direct or indirect. Direct speech repeats and quotes the exact words the original speaker used (even if that was the speaker). Indirect speech seeks to convey the meaning of the speech but doesn't use the original speaker's exact words. There are conflicting opinions on whether we consider direct speech a form of reported speech. Still, for our purposes, we will classify direct speech as a form of reported speech and look at the differences and implications for data and communication between direct and indirect speech.

When storing data, it is easy to assume that data would be considered direct speech. We use the computer to store the data input by a specific individual. Direct speech, as a direct quote and repeating of what was actually said, would align nicely with data recording. Especially from an accounting perspective, it is all just facts and numbers, so one would assume that the data should be considered a direct speech instance.

However, we ignore the systems and programs we have put into place to move data and transfer it, transforming it from one system to another. Even in data capture, when a trader enters something into their execution platform, they translate some real-world occurrence into the vocabulary of the execution system that has set options to choose from based on how the system was built and coded.

Interestingly enough, direct speech "is often used in informal conversations,"[†] when delivered without context, direct speech can be misleading or misunderstood. A famous example is a misused quote, taken out of context by (second president of the United States) John Adams, stating, "This would be the best of all possible worlds if there were no religion in it!" However, the full quote, in context, is "Twenty times, in the course of my late Reading, have I been upon the point of breaking out, This would be the best of all possible worlds if there were no religion in it!. But in this exclamation I should have been as fanatical as Bryant of Cleverly. Without Religion this World would be Something not fit to be mentioned in polite Company."

The context we can see significantly influences the interpretation of meaning for what is considered direct speech. Indirect speech, in contrast, typically does contain context. The reporting speaker includes situational context and will rephrase what they hear in their own words to provide proper meaning to the listener. For the John Adams quote, an indirect speaker may say, "Adams said in many of the things he has been reading, he was pressed about the climate of sectarian dogma and professed how the world would be worse off without religion."

If we consider data stored language, and that data is stored without context, using that data without context is akin to pulling quotes out of context and using them to support whatever perspective suits us falsely.

Bias

According to the catalog of bias,[‡] health science researchers identified 62 forms of bias specific to medical research as of the time of this writing. To help organize this, the researchers created a taxonomy that groups these into four main areas: conceptualization, selection, conduct, and reporting (dissemination). Ostensibly meant for health care and research studies,

---

[†] Accessed August 31, 2023, https://everydayspeech.com/sel-implementation/direct-speech-vs-indirect-speech-a-comprehensive-comparison-with-examples/.
[‡] Accessed January 19, 2023, https://catalogofbias.org/.

this listing still provides a helpful insight into biases that affect data and language interpretation.

In conceptualization, bias enters in through our individual world views—influenced by the CoP or CoPs we operate in—regarding how we look to interpret information. Confirmation bias is an excellent example of this, where we seek to interpret information in a way that supports the ideas or beliefs we already have. Selection-related biases influence how we collect information—effectively filtering or classifying what and how we collect information. Conduct biases involve interactions, such as when someone alters their behavior because they know they are being watched or observed (the Hawthorne effect). Finally, reporting or dissemination bias is how we present information—so the use of spin or rhetoric influences the eventual interpretation. Network effects are an excellent example of this kind of bias—where we broadcast one anomaly event repeatedly so that it seems like it is a normal occurrence versus the fringe or minority occurrence it is.

These groupings are subjective and influenced by the focus of the researchers. But the work is helpful in multiple ways. First, it is highly illustrative that bias has a broad impact and can impact even highly scientific and mathematical areas. Second, one could view the groupings as more simply what, where, why and how.

Bias can exist in the information we consume. Alternatively, in consuming information, we change that information using our biases. And we are biased in where we tend to go for information. Bias manifests in many ways. Even in light of overwhelming information, expert bias can lead people to ignore that information because *they know better.* In recording something, bias may lead someone not to include information—either because they have a bias that they should already know the missing information or because they do not deem it *important enough.*

A BARC Business Intelligence and Analytics Survey in 2022 found that "58 percent of our respondents say their companies base at least half of their regular business decisions on gut feel or experience, rather than on data and information."[§] Further, "39 percent of companies state that

---

[§] Accessed November 15, 2023, https://bi-survey.com/business-decisions-gut-feel?ref=blog.cads.ai.

gut feel/experience is good enough to make decisions with no relevant information."[5] Especially when data counters someone's expertise and experience, they tend not to trust the data, and instead go with their gut. Expertise is an excellent basis for evaluating recommendations. Still, the inherent bias can blind individuals—experts especially—in light of sudden environmental changes or simple evolutionary changes where that expertise may no longer be relevant or misleading.

When we look at Communities of Practice, one can see that one CoP will tend to have certain biases that are different from other CoPs, even if they interact directly. To prevent offending other groups, we often call this a *different perspective*. However, different perspectives are usually expressions of bias. Information relevant to one CoP may not apply to another. In the case of the front office versus the back office, there is an implicit bias toward exchange being important—and the view of information and data through that lens, as opposed to depository settlement. Even when considering settlement, the front office will be biased toward central counterparty (CCP) settlement processes instead of depository (CSD) processes.

Coupled with CoP, it should be evident that expertise impacts bias similarly. We may gain expertise from participation in a CoP, but it is much more an individual property. Individual expertise influences the interpretation of meaning and how an individual attempts to decipher meaning.

The acronym SME for example, to many, is shorthand for *subject matter expert*. Yet, for others, it refers to *small and medium enterprises*. Given the context in which we use the acronym, one would think that a reasonable person would know which of these concepts it refers to. However, expertise can cause one to ignore context and misinterpret meaning. I sat in a presentation concerning market infrastructure issues, and more than once, they highlighted that the inclusion of *SMEs* was critical to success. Based on my expertise, I assumed this referred to subject matter experts, which made practical sense even given the context. It was another hour into the discussion when someone said

---

[5] Accessed November 15, 2023, https://bi-survey.com/decision-making-no-information.

"small and medium enterprises" until I realized my incorrect assumption, and this realization changed the meaning of the entire conversation for me.

"In some cases, experts overextend themselves because their trespass is into an area of expertise close enough to their own that a stretch of professional judgement seems reasonable."[4] Where two experts confer in two related but different domains, it is easy for them to become blind to the biases in understanding each CoP individual carries. Given their respective levels of expertise, each will tend not to give deep explanatory information, expecting the other to understand. Witness an expert in brokerage settlement operations talking with a custody settlement operations expert, discussing trade settlement. In multiple working groups over the years, I have listened to both sides arguing about how the solution to settlement problems is to use the FIX message format (the broker) while the custody expert insists on ISO15022 formats. Until we force them to walk through, step by step, the processes they follow to settlement, both sides have assumed the processes were the same and comparable.

Interestingly enough, when both sides admit that the processes are different and have different needs, one or both continue to insist they are "similar enough" and that no differences exist. And because we regard them as experts, they continue propagating erroneous information.

In-Group, Out-Group Bias

While I focused on expertise bias related to CoP, I did want to call attention to a specific bias that is more of a socio-psychological nature. Part of belonging to a CoP includes shared culture. And the identification of oneself as *belonging* is itself a complex concept. It is "rooted in the tendency of human beings to discriminate others based of their affiliations and categorize them as either members of their own group (i.e., in-group members) or as members of other groups (i.e., out-group members) (see Turner and Tajfel 1986, for Social Identity Theory)."[5]

Some biases come into play when we identify with one group over another. Again, I will turn to sports as a simple example. If we identify with one team, say Fulham FC of the English Premiership, and find out someone we are interacting with is a Chelsea FC supporter—a rival club a mile up the road, there is a natural tendency to have a more negative viewpoint of what they say. We may perceive, without any intent, slights, and insults or distrust facts or statistics that they quote. The fragmented political environment globally points to this as well. A simple exchange where both parties engage and learn from each other on a noncontroversial topic can be suddenly ruined by finding out the other supports a different political party.

So when we talk about CoP, we should be sure to understand that there are influences on meaning based not just on expertise but also on in-group and out-group biases that influence interpretation and believability. "[O]ut-group members [are] associated with positive traits to a lesser extent (e.g., Dovidio, Kawakami, Johnson, Johnson, and Howard 1997; Dovidio and Gaertner 2000) and deemed less trustworthy than in-group members (e.g., Insko, Schopler, Hoyle, Dardis, and Graetz 1990; Insko, Schopler, and Sedikides 1998)."[6] These biases influence the use and promotion of language—our power dynamics issue—where one group, say a supervising authority, does not trust the groups they are supervising due to these biases and fault the language and mistrust the data from these groups.

Influence of Bias on the Interpretation of Context

Knowledge may lead us to believe that context would counter bias. However, the interaction of bias and context is not so clean and simple. Knowledge of context differs from how that context is interpreted or presented. That is to say, bias can influence the context itself.

Bias influences context, which we need to interpret stored or uttered information properly. This influence may initially seem recursive—but instead, context should be viewed in light of the bias that may exist, much like we discussed about perspective. If we look at the linguistic, social, and physical context, all of these contain aspects of potential bias.

Bias in Stored Data

Storing data does not somehow remove biases. Indeed, stored data will be heavily influenced by those who created it, the primary influencer being the CoP that created and stored it. Whether the data is in a database or a written document in a file folder, it is recorded as an expression of the viewpoint and understanding of the person who created it.[**] The heavy use of jargon will also impact data, especially in financial services.

Any biases in the creation of data will continue to exist—whether it be confirmation or selection bias—or biases based on subject matter expertise and the CoP to which the person belongs. Especially in the latter case (expertise and CoP-influenced biases), there is a greater potential that not all the pertinent information will be stored and saved—because there will be the tendency to expect anyone using that data to infer and assume the extra contextual bits of information that surround what was stored.

As mentioned previously, context typically does not exist in stored data. Bias and context work hand in hand to confound the data manager in being able to merge datasets or share data across boundaries—especially when those boundaries are historically poorly defined and resist quantitative or clear definition.

Let's refer back to the difference in terminology between the front and back office in derivatives where the front office used price, and the back office used rate to describe the same concept. The front office has a bias where the data labeling and definition will match their language: *price*, and they will store the data in a field named *price*. The definition will correspond to "the price at which the trade was executed." The front office's context assumes that the price is constantly changing, and they express this through a rate in the case of certain derivatives instruments. However, the members of that CoP understand that we could express the price for some other financial instrument as a number, such as in the case of the price of equity shares.

[**] Using a singular person here for simplicity's sake. But it could be the collaborative work of a group, output from a process or function, or otherwise.

For the back office, however, the price is the total value of the outstanding contract divided by the size. The fixed rate, which the front office knew as the *price*, is now considered a static variable with a different conceptual and contextual meaning. These differences in interpretation are informed by the goals and purpose of the particular CoP—as raised in the section above on context, the goal of the particular context is critical to know and works hand in hand with the biases that exist in operating directly in that environment.

There typically needs to be some data management practice within the organization to store data. *Business users* will usually need to interact with technologists to structure a database, decide what data to store, and create data definitions for the data to be stored.

Even in the face of an existing data program with defined terms and rules set on what data means, it is still a reality that those storing data could be using the storage mechanism but assigning their own meaning to the data outside of what is *officially* noted.

One simple example is where a CoP has to use a pre-established storage solution that may not contain all the necessary fields. Instead of modifying the dataset, they identify data points in the storage solution they usually wouldn't use. Effectively seeing these as otherwise useless, they repurpose those data fields for similar but different data and make the necessary adjustments outside of the official system. The decision is particularly destructive, as the biased data is comingled and mixed with data that retains the original meaning.

Bias in Reading Other Data

Bias is stored inherently in any data, as we have discussed. We keep that data with an implied but unspecified context based on the people and processes directly involved. One half of the problem is that the *speaker* storing the data does so with the intention that they—and their CoP—will be utilizing that data and will understand the meaning when accessing it later.

Data is not limited to use and access by one specific CoP. The *listeners* can be broad and varied as to why someone is accessing certain data matters as much as what CoP they identify with. Especially in cases where the data inquirer has a specific purpose or goal, this can lead to their biases reading unintentional meaning into data and making false correlations between particular data.

Confirmation bias—a form of conceptualization bias discussed earlier, can lead to one only searching for data that supports a predetermined condition or interpreting data in a way that fits the desired narrative. People routinely do not dig out—or will actively ignore—information that does not support their preconceived biases. However, the data does not have to have a bias for interpretation biases to occur. An oft-cited interpretation bias example is creating a false causality where data shows that ice cream sales and increases in crime rates occur in tandem, and the resulting interpretation is that ice cream sales cause higher crime.

One would think that interpretation bias would have little impact when dealing with hard numbers, such as in financial services. Joseph Berardino, former chief executive of Arthur Anderson, was quoted in his congressional testimony on the Enron collapse that "Many people think accounting is a science, where one number, namely earnings per share, is the number, and it's such a precise number that it couldn't be two pennies higher or two pennies lower. I come from a school that says it really is much more of an art."[7] In *Why Good Accountants Do Bad Audits*, the authors illustrate that auditors working for a firm would more highly value a company. In contrast, those working in roles more critical of the company would value the company significantly lower while using the same exact data and financial records.[8]

Another study in 2013 "found that an auditor who has knowledge of unaudited balances and identifies the most relevant piece of information pertaining to the fluctuation only selected the correct cause 33 percent of the time. In contrast, auditors who form expectations without unaudited balances were not only significantly more likely to recognize the most relevant piece of additional information, but also, when they did so, they correctly identified the cause 88 percent of the time."[9]

These studies illustrate that when examining data, individuals bring their own bias and can significantly misinterpret it even when removing source context and bias. It is reasonable to extend this further and expect that when analyzing data from outside one's CoP, we can misinterpret context and intent, leading to incorrect data use.

We can complicate this further by raising the issue of data translation from one CoP to another, where data passes through middleware based on rules created by business experts.

> Birbili states that when we collect data in one language and subsequently present the findings in another, the translators involved must make translation-related decisions [www.ncbi.nlm.nih.gov/pmc/articles/PMC2705066/#R1].[9] These decisions, she contends, have a direct impact on the research validity and are directly related to the autobiography of translators, the linguistic competence of the translators, the translators' knowledge of the people under study, and the circumstances in which the translation takes place [1 p.1]. Beck and colleagues also note that the translators' cultural experience, knowledge, and qualifications influence the quality of the translations [www.ncbi.nlm.nih.gov/pmc/articles/PMC2705066/#R8]. To assume that translators are merely transmitters of neutral messages is likely to inhibit access to understanding the translation process and the emerging data [www.ncbi.nlm.nih.gov/pmc/articles/PMC2705066/#R9]. Researchers must be cognizant of the translators' "material circumstances" relating to their perceived power and, to an extent, expertise over the target group [www.ncbi.nlm.nih.gov/pmc/articles/PMC2705066/#R9].[10]

The effect of a translator's bias becomes increasingly important in the interconnected social system of financial services and the continued drive for automation and straight-through processing. Even outside of analytics, a significant amount of data is picked up from one database or source, transformed, and deposited in another database under the ownership of a different CoP performing different functions and processes.

In trying to solve data management issues, data managers have yet to recognize the inherent conflict in the goals they are working toward—which mirrors the irony of language itself. People mean to communicate through language, but because it evolves, it is harder to communicate as boundaries and interactions expand. Consider the expectation of data managers to bring together the vast quantity of data stored throughout an enterprise or the task of standards setters to standardize data across diverse communities that interact over a process that is effectively similar to an assembly line.

In this assembly line, individual parts are assembled and passed on to the next stage, which is not concerned with the first set of individual parts. Their parts are parts from multiple sources. Further, we strip out pieces added in previous steps that we no longer need in later steps. When building an automobile or other physical object, this is more tangible. When we add a door to a car frame in assembly, we do not disassemble the door first. It becomes just a single item—a door. The minor differences in individual components can significantly influence the quality of an overall assembled component.

Assembling a car is a highly complex process, with contingencies for supply chain issues that can occur, resulting in multiple sources for the same parts. Interestingly, two doors may be assembled from different parts or sources and still be considered fungible. While fungible one component may be of a different quality than another, resulting in two *exact* cars having different overall quality levels. The fungibility of the *same data* can be even more disparate in data. There are the same concerns about quality from two different sources. Further, the *same* data from two different sources can be quite different, not necessarily related to the inherent quality of the data but the context and source, where the biases and context of the CoP result in implied information that is not captured and correctly translated further down the line.

CHAPTER 6

The False Premise

Everybody Needs to Know Everything

There are multiple issues with the idea that everyone needs to, or should be able to, know or access everything. The first issue we tie to a concern with expertise. Just because someone has access to information—and may understand some of that information—does not make them an expert or able to use that information properly. Notwithstanding Dunning-Kruger effect,[*][1] we, as individuals, can tend to believe that, because we are *smart*, we can understand everything. This may be a more acute problem for experts, as "One of the most common errors experts make is to assume that because they are smarter than most people about certain things, they are smarter than everyone about everything."[2]

"Facts, as experts know, are not the same as knowledge or ability."[3] The rise of the internet and Google highlights this best. People are driven to self-diagnose their ailments and argue with their doctor about what their symptoms mean. Even ignoring Sturgeon's law about 90 percent of all things on the internet being crap, and the amount of false or misleading information pretending to be medical advice that exists, only a trained doctor has the expertise to interpret the facts of a medical diagnosis than the individual who typed some symptoms into Google. Of course, there are examples where individuals turned out to be correct, and their doctors were wrong. But we forget that these are examples born out of confirmation and selection bias—that they

---

[*] Named after David Dunning and Justin Kruger, research psychologists at Cornell University in a 1999 study that found that the dumber you are, the more confident you are that you're not actually dumb.

are outliers. Overall, the doctor as the expert is likely better than the individual in diagnosis.

Allowing everyone to know everything, even if it is practical, ignores the aspect of expertise and ability to understand and use the information properly. Understanding something takes more than just reading information. When handed information, there is the issue of having the ability to use it properly.

In today's day and age, the amount of information readily available on the internet and in books at your local library can enable a layperson to amass all the information necessary to fix a car. So, why do mechanics still exist? The simple answer is that bringing a malfunctioning car to a mechanic is easier and less time-consuming. But why is this so? It is the underlying expertise. A mechanic can diagnose a car problem quicker and more efficiently. They likely have seen the same problem before, can get the correct diagnosis on the first try, and will fix it more quickly.

Meanwhile, someone with lots of information but no expert knowledge will likely misdiagnose the problem multiple times before stumbling upon the correct diagnosis. In fixing the problem, the mechanic may use their expert knowledge to know that a simple wrench turn or replacement of a single part will fix it. The information-heavy nonexpert will likely try one solution after another, perhaps even replacing entire sections, before possibly landing on the correct solution. Or, more likely, give up and bring it to a real expert—the mechanic— to get it fixed properly.

The Hot Tub and the Heat

Here, I will break down and admit that I fall into the ailment of being a Google-fueled expert in things myself. Two recent examples came to mind as I was re-editing this section.

First, the 15-year-old plug-in 110-volt hot tub I have started tripping the GFCI outlet. The tripping has happened before. Twice. I replaced the pump the first time, and all was fine after using Google. The second time, it was the control box, which I also replaced, and it started working again through Google and then the sales help desk. So, here we go, loaded with experience and knowledge—not necessarily expertise—and I decided to fix it again myself.

First, I was not confident it was the pump. But all signs and repeated Googling pointed toward that. So I spent another few hours determining what pump I precisely needed as a replacement—and trying to find the least expensive one. I ordered the pump, it arrived, and I set about installing it. Finished, and fingers crossed, I turned on the tub and—surprise—it worked!

But, still, the water wasn't moving much, and the heat didn't go up. So, investigating more online revealed I purchased a 1/15 HP pump, not a 1 HP pump. I suspected this to be the problem, even though all the advertisements insisted that horsepower has nothing to do with anything and that 1/15 should work fine. After those hours, I spent a few more hours finding a new 1 HP pump and ordered it. A different pump than I ordered arrived, but the salespeople online insisted it was the same. I decided to ignore price differences at this point, given the sunk cost of hours already.

After another couple of hours of uninstalling the old pump, re-installing the new pump, and filling the tub, fingers crossed, the pump turned on. And the water was moving as expected. And the water was warming up. It's likely that if I called an expert to come and work on it, I would have spent less than the day's worth of hours, not to mention over a week of delay, and would not have had the level of uncertainty that still persists. It may break down at any point, for all I know.

At the same time, the heat in the bathroom isn't working. It's a radiant system, and I know enough that air in the radiator can keep the water from circulating. I've bled other sections before to some success and some failures. Following my googling advice, I bled the section to no avail. Doing something else advised online, I sent 5 gallons of water into my basement due to a pressure backflow. I've likely spent 10 hours working on this, and the heat still isn't on. My wife is not happy with me. The plumber came and said that the circulating pump was bad. So, all my efforts were in vain.

> I'm an expert in many things. But I still need a reminder now and then to tell me I'm not an expert in many more things and should call someone who is.

Specialists who must interact for a grander goal are usually aware of their role. "When we build skyscrapers, we do not expect the metallurgist who knows what goes into a girder, the architect who designs the building, and the glazier who installs the windows to be the same person… each expert, although possessing some overlapping knowledge, respects the professional abilities of many others and concentrates on what he or she knows best."[4] There is an informal social mechanism here where the expert specialists involved know where their dependencies exist and respect that.

When specialists in a social system do not have this awareness—either because of the opacity of the social system or lack of clear divisions, this mutual interaction and respect can break down. Further, when we seek expert input outside of a specific goal, where dependencies are unclear, fewer barriers keep an expert from straying from their core competence. "Unfortunately, when experts are asked for views outside their competence, few are humble enough to remember their responsibility to demur."[5]

It is a natural human desire to want to know everything. It is difficult to go against human nature and acknowledge that we cannot know everything, especially when we are wrong.

Data Democratization

What Is It?

Data democratization is the concept that we should enable everyone in an organization or system to access all available data, regardless of their technical ability or specialization, without outside help. There is a belief, rightly or wrongly, that gatekeepers of data create bottlenecks in the sharing and acquiring of data that would prove useful or even necessary to a broader audience. Access to this data would, ostensibly, provide for better decision making. It usually involves goals such as breaking down data silos, building a data culture, improving the customer experience, and empowering employees.

Data democratization is not a new concept. In 2003, *business intelligence* advances were heralding the democratization of data. Data democratization's roots go earlier, since the early days of the personal computer, where data was in mainframes and especially hard to access, outside of specific and usually expensive requests for reports.

Data democratization in modern practice typically focuses on systems architecture and tools that enable anyone in an organization to access and use data, including access to tools for data analytics that are accessible and understandable by nontechnical people. Lists for successful data democratization projects typically contain visualization tools, open data platforms, data catalogs, and analytics tools. While there is an acknowledgment of traditional information technology adoption challenges—usually described as instilling a *data culture* and providing training—this is still viewed as a purely technological solution venture.

On the con side, the main issues raised tend to revolve around security and compliance concerns. These are entirely valid. Regulations around GDPR[†] and CCPA[‡] protect against misusing personally identifiable information (PII). There are additional and valid security concerns related to PII, sensitive company information, and general data security requirements on why we should avoid democratizing sensitive data.

Many data professionals view data democratizing as one of their main goals—and technology vendors are entirely on board in pushing the narrative of its promise. Aside from the security-related issues noted, there seems to be a general alignment that all other data should be accessible and useable. The benefits from various providers and chief data officers generally surround better collaboration, more reliable data,

[†] General Data Protection Regulation is a European Union-based regulation for information privacy.
[‡] California Consumer Protection Act is a personal information protection Act for residents of California in the United States.

saving time and money, and more data-driven decision making (instead of *gut* decisions).

At the same time, the barriers seem somewhat similar to the topics we discuss here. A blog on *Opendatasoft* lists barriers as "data means different things to different people," "data is often siloed," "data remains in the hands of experts," and "organizational culture does not encourage sharing."[6] These concepts are not unique and permeate the general data democratization ecosystem. Siloed data, lack of centralization, and the "single source of truth" is noted by David Bunting in a ChaosSearch Blog,[7] and an Actian article highlights silos and that semantic layers are not enough.[8]

It should not be surprising that the barriers to data democratization align with the challenges applied linguistics seeks to resolve. Different definitions, silos, and a perception of protectionism by organizations and expert groups all point to the basics of misunderstanding and communication barriers between Communities of Practice.

The *Opendatasoft* blog also summarizes a presentation by Olivier Thereaux, head of research and development at the Open Data Institute, proposing "we need to understand these differences and work to create a definition of data that covers all its potential uses."[9]

Now, one can take two different interpretations of that statement —either it is speaking abstractly, and that there needs to be a shared definition of what *data* the concept means, or it is more specific in that data definitions for something must be aligned. Hence, a single definition of a term covers all its potential uses.

Hopefully, readers will agree that this should not be one of the goals in the latter case. Trying to create a single source of truth or enforcing a homogeneous definition of a term covering all uses is problematic in light of the language differences and different perspectives across CoP.

In the abstract sense, what Thereaux talks about, what data is and what it is for, differs across users and types. Further, Thereaux qualifies data democratization as data needing access by those who need it.[10] This view is a bit more nuanced than the prevailing generalization and implications. "By those who need it" shifts the idea from "data should be accessed by everyone" to "data should be accessed by those that can use it." A key aspect of being able to use data is being able to understand and correctly interpret it.

Does Everyone Agree That Data Should Be Democratized?

I have quoted Langefors before, but it bears repeating here:

> Information systems theory has, since its beginning in the early 1960s, been facing a contradiction. One of its main visions was that data in the system had to be available to "everybody" (Langefors 1961, #29, 1963, #37). But it was soon detected that a set of data does not inform everybody (the "infological equation." Langefors 1966, #1). It had to be concluded that efficiently designed information systems had to be structured as a network of communicating more or less separate subsystems based on local data systems. This insight took a surprisingly long time to gain recognition in the data profession, as well as, for instance, in accounting.
>
> Even when, in the 1980s, small local systems came to be fairly common, this was in many cases due to the emergence of inexpensive micro-computers, rather than to an understanding of the often local character of data.[11]

And further:

> "And, with the maturing of the technology of connecting small computers to form networks, one has begun again to talk about making all data accessible to everybody. We conclude that there is still lacking the understanding that some data are only intelligible to restricted groups of people. This suggests that there is need for case studies, in order to reach and disseminate a more concrete understanding of this aspect.
>
> It is often stated, for example, by data managers, that the popping up of isolated local systems will lead to chaos. Leaving aside the fact that some amount of chaos may be useful, we point out that keeping isolated such data as are in in any case

unintelligible outside a limited context can't by itself generate chaos. Of course, such data as have to be used in several locations, but those only, must be subject to integrated management—but this should not be done indiscriminately."[12]

It impresses me how well these principles and observations have held up over 50 or more years. Additionally, while Langefors does not explore linguistics specifically, he rests heavily upon the basis of socio-technical, and organizational behavior theories that closely align with sociolinguistic themes of Communities of Practice, expert understanding, and language intelligibility.

I continue to be somewhat disappointed by the technology community that seems to pay little heed to the nontechnical factors, aside from viewing them as barriers which, through better technology, on the one hand, could resolve and some level of behavior modification training for those that resist their brand of change. I hesitate to be too critical here, though, as the technology side has most definitely shifted in incorporating users in the development process, a focus on understanding goals and needs, the understanding of buy-in up front, and that the purpose of technology is to provide a solution for an actual human to somehow interact with and gain value. Still lacking is a broader understanding of Socio-Technical Theory,[13] and how it inter-relates with the potential use of applied linguistic tools and socio-organizational sciences.

However, there remains an issue within technology efforts and organizational systems of seeing both the trees and the forest. The general approach to framing, explaining, and discussing data democratization presents an issue. As mentioned above, data democratization, as a concept, has been simplified to give access to all data (except that secure, sensitive, PII-type data) to anyone and everyone. Inherent in that simplified view are assumptions about the data and the users. Data assumptions include ignoring linguistic variety and decrying the existence of data silos. User assumptions ignore expertise—predominately through the premise that technological wrangling can make anything intelligible to anyone.

This argument is not against data democratization within a bounded and specific context and the possible potential and realized benefits. The benefits and value of open data to the global community are easy to document. However, there is no discussion within limited contextual implementations of data democratization but as a complete and whole end goal for all data. The concept that all data should be inherently accessible to everyone leads toward implementation assumptions. But if we adjust the idea and conceptual view of data democratization to something more aligned with Thereaux's "for those that need it" and tighten it up with socio-technical views, perhaps we can describe what data democratization should be a bit differently.

Perhaps our view of data democratization should be identifying the data that belongs to a Community of Practice that is used or otherwise required by other Communities of Practice within their social system and enabling access and understanding for those that can effectively use it.

Here, we capture that not all data will be intelligible to those outside of a specific CoP, and that is OK. There is an acknowledgment that data silos exist (as defined through Communities of Practice), and this is OK. Referring back to the example of specialists building a skyscraper—most of the information and data any of those specialists use would be noise. Only the relevant data that needs to be shared—and translated to make it usable—is shared. Where notations specific to plumbing exist on plans, the mason doesn't interpret them independently; they bring the plumber back to answer questions about their expertise. It shifts the focus from broad cultural changes and education toward language translation and preserving linguistic variety versus the imposition of some homogeneous refactoring of an entire social system's data and language.

This inherent acknowledgment of knowledge separation is less respected in many industries, especially in technology. The lack of respect, however, is no indictment of technology professionals. I know technology and data professionals are all sensitive to the business, individual, and cultural issues that impact the delivery of technical and data solutions. To the point of this book, there remains a gap, and something is missing, or there would still not be significant challenges and difficulties in implementing technology and data projects. But offering data democratization as an answer should instead open up more questions about what we are trying to solve—data access for everyone or making sure the right people are in the room to explain what their data means instead of assuming we already know just because we can access it.

CHAPTER 7

Granular Data as a Red Herring

> A red herring is a misleading statement, question, or argument
> meant to redirect a conversation away from its original topic.[*]

I explored some challenges related to granularity in the previous
examples regarding dogs. In that example, we looked at how, starting
with some general concept, the granularity underneath still presented
a problem regarding the breadth and depth one must plumb. Further,
the requirements of the prevailing CoP dictate the specific direction of
that granularity. Additionally, each CoP has its own biases, which can
conflict as one gets more specific regarding the relevance of granularity.
That is, not at all granular information is relevant to all CoPs.

In the discussion of *trade*, we also examined that what any term
infers beyond the basic definitions depends on the context and the CoPs
involved in any particular activity. The activity of the function and
processes have an impact on the definition, as well as the different CoPs
involved. As we partly define CoPs by the specialized processes they
perform for their functional goals, this should make sense. But what if
we start at the granular level instead—at the *atomic* building blocks of
any assembled data set?

There has been a renewed focus on "granular data" to combat the
challenge of multiple definitions for any single term or multiple terms
with similar definitions. The theory is that by deconstructing complex
data down to the individual discrete data points and then formally
and rigidly defining them, one can eliminate the different definitions
and agree upon a single term where multiple may exist for the same
definition.

---

[*] Accessed August 31, 2023, www.grammarly.com/blog/red-herring-fallacy/.

The idea is to remove any single data point from any surrounding context. Without the nuance of context, it should exist in some pure form, like single electrons, protons, and neutrons, which are discrete things we can assemble in different combinations to create more complex objects.

In trade finance, a *price* is just some number corresponding to the value of some other object. Further, it is just a number at an even more granular level. Assuming that you could isolate the data concept of *price* and define the concept at a granular level, the expectation is that any data with a *price* label would then be able to be treated the same way, regardless of where it exists.

Following this method, we would follow the same methodology for each data point in any trade or transaction. The entities on either side of the trade, the quantity, and the asset or object of the trade all would exist as pure granular data elements defined outside the actual context of the trade itself. Therefore, by re-assembling the individual elements, there should be a "single version of the truth," conceptually removed from context, and therefore have purity of meaning.

Consider the sentence, "I never said she stole my money." This fairly popular linguistic meme shows up regularly on linguistics forums on Reddit and elsewhere. Generally, the linguistic game this sentence results in creates at least seven different meanings and potentially has as many as twice that.

Let us start with the assumption that every word in the sentence has a single definition and meaning.

I	The nominative singular pronoun, used in referring to oneself, the person speaking, writing, or otherwise communicating.
Never	Not ever; at no time.
Said	Simple past tense and past participle of say (to utter or pronounce, to express in words).
She	The female person or animal being discussed or last mentioned; that female.

(Continued)

(*Continued*)

Stole	Simple past tense of steal (to take [the property of another or others] without permission or right, especially secretly or by force).
My	A form of the possessive case of I used as an attributive adjective.
Money	Any circulating medium of exchange, including coins, paper money, and demand deposits.

Now, we then follow this with different articulations that stress different words within the sentence;

1. *I* never said she stole my money.
2. I *never* said she stole my money.
3. I never *said* she stole my money.
4. I never said *she* stole my money.
5. I never said she *stole* my money.
6. I never said she stole *my* money.
7. I never said she stole my *money*.

In example 1, in stressing "I," the sentence context implies that while the "she" in question may have stolen the protagonist's money, the speaker asserts that they never raised that accusation.

In example 2, by stressing *never*, the speaker asks if the target stole the money. There is not enough context, however, to indicate if she received the speaker's money, had not stolen it, or if the accusation had no merit at all.

In example 3, the nuance of emphasizing "said" gives some indication that she may have stolen the money in question, although the speaker herself did not make the accusation.

Example 4's stressing of "she" begins to make a clearer difference in the context of the situation, seeming to imply that someone stole the speaker's money, but the speaker suspects it was done by someone other than the target "she."

Example 5 implies that the she in question does have the speaker's money, but it was not stolen. Note that the context here differs from in example 2, where there is an open question on whether the target ever received any of the speaker's money.

For example 6, there is a clear accusation that the "she" did steal money, but it was not the speaker's.

Finally, in sentence 7, the speaker indicates that the target stole something, but not their money.

Additional emphasis on additional words can give even more context and clarification, mixing the different interpretations. So, how does this relate to storing granular data and common meaning? The premise behind breaking down complex data messages into granular data is to remove ambiguity by focusing on the individual elements. There is a focus on defining those elements as "concepts," separating any context that could result in more than one semantic meaning.

By trying to reduce any element to a "concept," the idea is that it will possess only one meaning. "Meaning is the cornerstone of language, since people communicate principally to convey meaning."[1] It would follow, then, that limiting any word to a single meaning in a granular data approach should simplify the data communication problem. But what those focusing on granular data miss is that "Meaning is more than a definition in a dictionary; it is also found in a context."[2] Further, "looking at words alone can lead to ambiguity, but context can provide critical information to identify the correct meaning."[3]

The depth of definition required begins to become highly complex when communicating outside the confines of one's Community of Practice. Just because something is a trade, many different types of trade can impact the intent. Who the entities involved in a transaction are is relevant to how we treat any trade. What type of asset or object is in a trade also affects how we interpret the trade and what actions may occur.

Defining each granular data point opens a virtual Pandora's box of issues. Regarding price—it is completely feasible that the price may be a percentage instead of a number. Further, price carries other nuances we must address, such as currency and number of decimal places—which have potential interacting dependencies and other external influencing factors.

Attempting to define data outside of context granularly ignores that all language—and therefore data —exists within some context. Sentence assembly is within its own context. This higher-level context speaks to the use case, the intent of the speaker, and the nuance they encode. This context can change the definition of the sentence as a whole, as the interaction of the "granular data" with each other changes the intended meaning.

The other complexity is answering the question of how atomic should we go. While I mentioned protons, electrons, and neutrons as the "granular points" earlier, I ignored the further breakdown of these *atomic*-level elements. The challenge is that at some point, the individual granular bits lose relevance in answering higher-level questions. Further, the more granular one gets, the more specific—and divergent—one becomes away from the *parent* generic concept that shares commonality across a wider audience.

To define "granular data" is not a fool's errand. However, the current approaches seek to perform this exercise to remove language's complexity. Thus, the argument for "granular data" sits on par with any call for a monolinguistic "common financial services language" that encompasses the entire social system of financial services without regard to the individual CoPs and their individual languages, dialects, and jargon that differentiate them from each other.

However, in the end, pursuing data purity of meaning through a granular data approach is a red herring.

Granular Data for Regulatory Reporting

The realm of regulatory reporting typically discusses granularity. Instead of creating specific reports to speak to various oversight requirements of any particular regulator, the offer is that *all the data* just be given to a regulator. The assumption is that the provision of *all the data* enables regulators to query and craft the investigative reports they require.

But, as noted above, data without context lacks meaning. It is not just the source of the data that provides context or the situation in which we create data. The original data assembly also provides context—the data collection as a single utterance infers meaning.

It becomes questionable if two similar trades, removed from all other contexts, would be appropriate to compare without the sources and evaluate the situational context in the trade execution. If the trade sizes are similar, but one firm is significantly larger and has considerably more buying power, it may speak to the smaller firm's trade to contain more risk in comparison. Further, the goal of the comparison (i.e., the reason for the oversight) also influences what contextual information may or may not be important. The firm context would be important to include if the goal is to judge the undertaken risk. However, the trading firm context would be less relevant if the goal is to track overall activity in a particular asset.

It can be a fair complaint that because there are so many different regulations for different purposes, firms tend to report the same information multiple times for various reasons. So the argument goes, why not just give all the information once and let the regulators assemble the data they need as they see fit? However, this would require firms to provide multiple levels of context in a massive amount of data. Across different firms, there would be variations between meaning and context, especially with the data meant to satisfy multiple different goals. The amount of ambiguity introduced would make deriving comparative meaning difficult, if not impossible, and likely lead to misleading results and interpretation.

CHAPTER 8

Practical Pragmatics—A Primer for Later

Sometimes, we describe pragmatics as how context affects meaning. This definition oversimplifies pragmatics, especially when discussing context and semantics used within data management.

MacMahon explains pragmatics as follows:

> Pragmatics is typically defined in contrast with semantics. While both semantics and pragmatics are concerned with meaning, semantics deals with abstract and relatively stable meanings within the linguistic system, and pragmatics concerns itself with variable aspects of meaning which are derivable from utterances within contexts of use. As such, pragmatics can be, and often is interpreted, as covering a wide range of contextual factors, including, for some researchers, aspects of sociolinguistics, conversational turn-taking and narrative structure (see Traugott and Pratt 1980), and cognitive poetics (see Radwańka-Williams and Hiraga 1995).[1]

In another way, pragmatics is more concerned about communicating information within and across language boundaries. At the same time, semantics defines a specific thing within a specific context in a static environment.

If the reader has come this far, let us assume we can agree on some basic things:

- Multiple Communities of Practice exist within any particular industry.

- Those CoPs interact as individual language groups within a more extensive social system.
- There is a need for one CoP to communicate information (data) to another (one or multiple) CoP that has a different language.
- Data storage by one CoP has its own linguistic variety that differs from another CoP.
- Linguistic varieties exist between CoPs.

Today, data practices focus on semantics—that is, ensuring that there is a clear and agreed definition for a particular business element or bit of data that is a clear and agreed definition for a particular business element or bit of data to be stored. This definition will necessarily be the semantic meaning of a specific CoP, though this fact is not typically acknowledged, registered, or documented. The only other alternative is that the definition is so generic that its meaning becomes utterly ambiguous and unusable. The data stored directly by the particular CoP is also managed by that CoP and primarily serves the function for the systems and processes primarily serving the function for the systems and processes that the CoP performs.

Regardless, the problem we face is not the storage and use of data by the CoP that owns and defines its data. Our problem is when a CoP accesses data that is not their own but created, defined, or otherwise managed by a different CoP, such as when they are sent information or need to go elsewhere to gather information that they will then want to use for their purposes.

By definition, this is not a semantics problem. So data professionals bring in the concept of context, which they have bolted on with duct tape to a foundation with semantics at its core, as the solution to create additional static meanings as variants of the "one true" semantic meaning already established as the *primary*. For example, the front office system originally built the concept of *trade* into its data. When we add a mid or back-office system or organization, and a new definition of *trade* is discovered, it either will be forced into the existing meaning or a new context type will be added to the enterprise dictionary as a subtype of the original.

Examining something like the life cycle of a trade through the lens of CoP, we should see it is not purely a context problem either. It is a problem of dealing with variable meaning, affected by communicating across language boundaries of different CoPs with different social systems, biases, assumptions of meaning, intent, and context of use. By definition, the most significant problem we face as data managers is one of pragmatics. Yet, we insist on using the tools of semantics and biased context to try and solve it.

For a data manager, the key is ensuring that any data assembled comes from the same context, which includes the CoP perspective, the perspective of the listener, the context of the speaker (creator of the report, file, transaction, or other sent data), the situational context of the source data such that it matches the situational context of the intended need (where we destine the use of the data), and more. When we assemble data from multiple sources that do not share the same language and are from different contexts, a repeating ad hoc exercise to try and align this data into one of the supplied contexts is performed—or more often, some artificial context is created that mangles everything together in a way that different CoPs won't be too offended but will still need to learn this new context and try and translate it back to their own.

Thus, the only real way to accomplish this is to ensure that the data is stored so that all the needed contextual relationships are captured and associated with preserving context. When pulled, the data is associated with the context of the destination/listener. That the data is subsequently changed (as well as its context) should be recognized—and realized that it is not the same (contextually, meaning or otherwise) as the sourced data, other than in a very generic sense.

We pull information, then haphazardly look at it and make it fit with other data we have pulled and analyzed (normalizing it). We are then shoving it together in some consensus "harmonized way" that we can present as generally capturing some shared view based on the finalized medium and representation chosen (e.g., U.S. GAAP versus IFRS in XBRL or other). These "harmonized" terms become the basis for any data dictionary, and as the data project expands to take in more systems across an enterprise, we expect those systems to conform.

With each new conformity effort comes some recognition that there is a potential miscommunication and any number of terms, like *price*. The price we execute something at may be the same numerical value as it settles at in a later process, but we should not take it to mean the same thing. In the context of the original trade, the price has a different intent, inference, and use than the price during the final settlement. Therefore, while they may be relatable to each other, they should not be assumed to be stored in the same field with a common definition. But this is often not discovered until system, trade, or valuation errors occur.

We have looked at semantics, context, bias, CoP, and other influences on the interpretation of meaning. These individual pieces play a role in language interpretation, regardless of the speaker's intent or the intended original meaning of the component pieces (bits of data). Moving forward, one should consider this introduction to the concept of pragmatics. There is always more going on in any communication, especially between parties that belong to two different CoP. Any communication made in the environment can influence the interpretation of data—including previous interactions (especially ones that link to the current interaction), the specific context or performed use case, and the different perspectives the parties involved may be coming from.

CHAPTER 9

The Failure of (How) Technology (Is Applied)

Technology cannot solve our data management problems. Yet, you search for "data management solutions," and there are pages and pages of references that seem to paint the picture that software and systems are the answer to your data management problems.

These technology solutions promise to "break down data silos," "manage data across a diverse but unified data tier," and "integrate, transform and govern your data." Technology solutions are as prolific as they are diverse.

I'm sure most data managers found my proclamation provocative. But, I will soften that statement slightly and note that technology can and will *help* solve our data management problems. However, there are no technologies we can directly apply to the primary data problem related to language and readily fix cross-CoP-related issues.

Unfortunately, this is how technology solutions in the data space are marketed and positioned. Here are some of the claims about data management technology solutions:

> Data management solutions unify organizational data to improve trust, control, and access. They enable organizations to break down data silos, providing centralized locations for accessing, exploring, and working with all organizational data.
>
> Data management solutions can support multiple departments and use cases across the business. Modern solutions leverage data-driven intelligence and artificial intelligence (AI) to help organizations solve complex problems.[*]

---

[*]Accessed April 11, 2023, www.imperva.com/learn/data-security/data-management-solution/.

Support the global identification, linking and synchroniza-
tion of master data across heterogeneous data sources through
semantic reconciliation of master data.[†]

There are "unify your disparate sources of information," "creating
data driven insights," "effortlessly manage data across all tools in
one centralized location," "normalize data across a range of sources,"
"discover the full value of your data" and other claims.

Only the most naive data managers would assume that buying a
piece of technology would remove all their problems or issues. There
is truth in the fact that any available technology solutions can aid in
addressing the issues endemic to managing data. However, solutions fail
without understanding data as language, even as many data professionals
try to understand why.

Saussure likens language to a game of chess.[1] Each piece has a
particular function and role and predetermined movements. Yet, at the
same time, the value of each piece depends on its position on the
chessboard and its relative position to other pieces. However, the initial
rules about their function, role, and movements bind them. Moving
one chess piece does not just impact the one piece but affects the entire
system in value and options available.

If we liken the chess pieces to data, a finite, although complex, set of
information exists. It is still able to be stored and organized. However,
this approach ignores one aspect—a chess player intends to "bring about
a shift and thereby exert and action on the system, whereas language
premeditates nothing."[2] In the same way, a user has intent in the actions
they take, the data they create and use, and store. This action extends
to the entirety of the Community of Practice they operate in, as well.
Further, where data is used and exists in the overall social system of a
company or industry matters—its meaning and purpose change, just
like a chess piece moving across the board.

The basic meanings of language—and by association data—are
modified spontaneously by intent. Intent can be inferences, assumptions, or otherwise. It is what we see in the example of granular data

---

[†]www.gartner.com/reviews/market/master-data-management-solutions.

where "I did not say she stole my money." The statement's intent and the creator's assumptions profoundly impact meaning.

There is a certain irony in the technical approach to data and language, most exemplified in NLP, AI, and ML efforts, but even within simple data management, that ignores the implications of Saussure's chess pieces. Today, typically data is treated as just that—chess pieces —without considering the players acting on those pieces (pragmatics). Throughout the coming section, I'll explore the different data-related technologies and approaches and suggest where to insert the different applied linguistic concepts and tools already discussed and add value. There are also some criticisms of current approaches and established thinking that pertain to each.

Storage

Data is the stored language of different CoPs or language groups that enables long-term storage and preservation of information and facilitates communication across large populations. Data storage is as old as written language—one can point to clay and stone tablets, paper books, and even paintings as ways humans have stored information over the centuries.

More relevant to today's data challenges is the digitization that began with the advent of the computer—with punch cards, data tapes and reels, and the creation of data stores that preceded the modern database. There is some need to dive into the technical end of things when examining data storage concerning the issues we face about bias, context, and meaning, but I won't get deeply technical. As such, technologists may find me somewhat liberal with my discussion of the technologies at hand, structures of databases, and methodologies. But I will try to be as accurate as possible while remaining at a layperson's level of discussion.

A Brief History

Computerization necessarily requires data storage for computers to act on, present results, and even store those results. By the 1960s, mainframe computers based on COBOL mainly used the CODASYL (Conference on Data System Language) network model or the IMS (Information Management System) hierarchical model. These were very complicated systems focusing on the systems' functionality instead of human interaction.

As knowledge and talent grew, there was a need to have better search tools that human operators could use to access datasets directly. The concept of relational databases was born out of a series of papers by Edgar Codd, who was then at IBM. These relational database management systems (RDBM) were more flexible and efficient, especially for the growing nonmainframe computer world.

Normalization

Beginning in the 1970s, Edgar F. Codd proposed the concept of normalization for databases in a paper, "A relational model of data for large shared data banks."[3] The relational model aimed to reduce redundancy in databases, as at the time, reducing storage and computational requirements was highly desirable. Reduced redundant data also increases data quality by improving consistency and making managing databases easier.

Over the coming decade, Codd and others improved upon the concept, introducing additional "normal forms":

First Normal Form (1NF): This is the most basic level of normalization. In 1NF, each table cell should contain only a single value, and each column should have a unique name. The first normal form helps to eliminate duplicate data and simplify queries.

Second Normal Form (2NF): 2NF eliminates redundant data by requiring that each nonkey attribute be dependent on the primary key. This means that each column should be directly related to the primary key and not to other columns.

Third Normal Form (3NF): 3NF builds on 2NF by requiring that all nonkey attributes are independent of each other. This means that each column should be directly related to the primary key and not to any other columns in the same table.

Boyce-Codd Normal Form (BCNF): BCNF is a stricter form of 3NF that ensures that each determinant in a table is a candidate key. In other words, BCNF ensures that each nonkey attribute is dependent only on the candidate key.

Fourth Normal Form (4NF): 4NF is a further refinement of BCNF that ensures that a table does not contain any multivalued dependencies.

Fifth Normal Form (5NF): 5NF is the highest level of normalization and involves decomposing a table into smaller tables to remove data redundancy and improve data integrity.[‡]

Sixth normal form is usually considered more theoretical than practical. Third normal form is considered optimal enough for most applications.

Where data is consistently and repeatedly read or written, normalization helps increase data access speed and accuracy. This increase is because queries can target a small set of relevant tables containing necessary information without loading all the data.

Complex queries running against large sets of data typically lead to denormalization. By denormalizing the data, fewer joins (temporary links between related tables) must be performed during the query, making it more efficient for deep analysis of vast datasets.

RDBM and tools like the Structured Query Language (SQL) became the primary database methodology. As late as the early 2000s, when considering data storage, the main question was usually deciding among some database providers, like Oracle or Sybase. The thought of data was about a basic table and column-defined, spreadsheet-like form. The ultimate theoretical goal was attaining a relational set of tables

[‡]Accessed July 26, 2023, www.geeksforgeeks.org/normal-forms-in-dbms/.

expressed in "sixth normal form"—a state where we could no further break or reduce the data.

These databases, accessed using SQL, were often called SQL databases. Companies like Oracle and Sybase sold platforms that could create complex databases with various data management tools that improved data access and management. Further enhancements added in-memory denormalized data and normalized "stored" data, increasing performance and functionality.

The basis of RDBM was tables with rows. Meanwhile, a new methodology started gaining attention where data storage was columnar.[§] With increasing computer power, larger databases found better performance using the column-focused approach.

Another innovation was NoSQL, which came about as part of the growth of the early internet. NoSQL models are nonrelational and based on a group of distributed databases aligned with the internet model of different nodes and an ad hoc method of accessing and organizing the data over the distributed system.

NoSQL heralded the entry of "Big Data," coinciding with the commercialization of the internet, trivialization of computing power and limitations on storage capacities, and the recognition that data creation was at a geometric rate. In 2022, Petroc Taylor wrote:

> The total amount of data created, captured, copied, and consumed globally is forecast to increase rapidly, reaching 64.2 zettabytes[¶] in 2020. Over the next five years up to 2025, global data creation is projected to grow to more than 180 zettabytes. In 2020, the amount of data created and replicated reached a new high. The growth was higher than previously expected caused by the increased demand due to the COVID-19 pandemic, as more people worked and learned from home and used home entertainment options more often.
>
> Only a small percentage of this newly created data is kept though, as just 2 percent of the data produced and consumed in

---

[§]Model 204 (M204) may be considered a precursor, launched by IBM in 1972.
[¶]A zettabyte is one sextillion (10^{21}). In comparison, a terabyte is one million million (10^{12}).

2020 was saved and retained into 2021. In line with the strong growth of the data volume, the installed base of storage capacity is forecast to increase, growing at a compound annual growth rate of 19.2 percent over the forecast period from 2020 to 2025. In 2020, the installed base of storage capacity reached 6.7 zettabytes.[**]

The Next Stage of Data Storage

In contrast to the old question of choosing Oracle or Sybase for a storage solution, there was a recognition that there was value in better understanding data and finding ways to use it. Driven by companies like Google and Amazon, firms began to rethink what data meant to their organizations. In the past, data dictionaries and data element-level definitions were sufficient when creating a relational database. The relationships provided context for the semantic meaning of the rows, columns, and tables, which are typically purpose-built for particular functions.

This point is not insignificant. Even though Communities of Practice shared data, many databases were created by and for the use of a specific CoP. It was the core basis for computer systems and processes that CoPs utilized for their specific function. As noted above in the pragmatics section, any CoP defined its own data for use in its own databases that fueled their CoP-specific systems and processes mainly in a vacuum. But, as is the nature of social systems, the information wasn't destined to stay in that vacuum and needed to be communicated outside.

These data silos heralded the rise of *middleware* systems designed to take the output from one area and perform mapping to convert the data into the definitions of the destination system, ostensibly operated by a different CoP. Within a single company, systems stitched together in this way that, over time, turned into what many called a spaghetti web of interactions between different systems and databases that all had their own terms and definitions. In many cases, users of various systems often

---

[**]Accessed July 26, 2023, www.statista.com/statistics/871513/worldwide-data-created/.

did not have insight into where the data they used came from. Further, the technology owners of systems were unaware of which systems they received data from or where they sent it to!

The Spaghetti Web

In the late 1990s and early 2000s, ISO created a new messaging standard for international settlements called ISO15022.[††] ISO15022 replaced an older standard that had been around for 10 or 15 years, called ISO7775.

I was one of a handful of subject matter experts who belonged to the industry association ISITC NA, which brought together professionals from the different firms involved in the settlement process—brokers, global custodian banks, investment managers, and industry infrastructures like Central Securities Depositories. Over several years, the working group at ISITC NA created agreed market practices for constructing the new ISO15022 messages and using them to send information between the different organizations for the various processes.

As a result, the company asked me to lead the effort in moving from ISO7775 messaging to ISO15022 messaging. The information available to be sent via the new messages was vastly greater than the limited ISO7775 messages, so this required an end-to-end analysis of the system architecture and changes to core systems to support data storage and creation. In some cases, mainframe systems were affected, and the only solution was to hardcode COBOL copybooks because mainframes did not utilize relational databases.

However, the architecture discussion was the most telling experience illustrating the complexity of interconnected systems. All technology heads that owned any system within the organization got together in a conference room, and we began to trace the trade path through all the systems on a whiteboard. The spaghetti web quickly

---

[††]I discuss ISO15022, it's precursor, ISO7775, and the later ISO20022 in my previous book.

revealed itself. The discussions asked different system owners where they sent data or whose system they received data from.

At more than one point, arguments broke out when someone would state that they received data from (or sent data to) a particular system, and the system owner would categorically state that it was not true. The complexity and interrelation between systems, even for a single process, were so complex that even the expert owners of any one component were not aware of the dependencies they had on others or that others had on them. Sometimes, a system owner would refuse to believe a claim until someone brought physical proof to them at the next meeting.

Middleware still exists as a necessary tool in connecting disparate relational systems. However, there has been more centralization of such solutions, where solutions handle dozens of different connections across dozens of systems that need to interact. However, they operate very much on a direct translation basis, for the most part. From an applied linguistic perspective, business analysts act as subject matter experts in identifying and translating the required data from the source system into the terminology and form of the destination. This translation was usually only one-way, with the analyst tasked to understand the context and semantic meaning of the source data and ensure that it matched the required context, intended use, and semantics of the destination. Middleware traditionally uses a semantics-based methodology with context bolted on, if at all.

Middleware, therefore, can be difficult and expensive to maintain over time. Expertise changes, and key information lies buried in business and functional requirement documents rather than being part of the system and data itself. Language is not static. The omission of why there is a logical mapping from one point to another and the downstream or upstream impact of changes is typically not evident. Middleware can tend to be more of a static approach for a repetitive process, so when those processes evolve or change, it becomes harder and harder to adapt. It also is not as effective for enterprise-wide analysis and information sharing.

All these different factors around existing data management systems had data managers looking toward the promises of big data and the data warehouse. Massive data stores that everything could be dumped into and then sifted for insights, analysis, and unknown correlations appeared to be a final solution to the ever-increasing data stream, especially with the capturing of more frequent unstructured data.

The view is that data warehouses and data lakes are technological innovations that could take advantage of leaps in computing power, lower storage costs, deliver data democratization, and provide deep analytical insights. The more data, the better, as computer scientists and the newly emerging data scientists would be able to use this newly expanded computing power to tackle the Tower of Babel problem that has plagued humanity since the invention of language.

Is That a Data Lake or Warehouse?

Data warehouse, as a term, is usually the term most laypeople will use to refer generically to any large data store that is not a relational database. However, some differences are significant for data professionals, as any language nuance tends to be.

Data warehouses should mean large data stores that are considered structured. Data lakes, in contrast, are large stores of unstructured data.

So, then, what is the difference between structured and unstructured data?

Unstructured data is typically raw data—data that hasn't been processed through some set of business rules to provide business alignment—either by aligning with defined semantics or context or tagging the data with relationships to other data. Examples of unstructured data could be documents, such as Word or PDF documents, especially those that have not been tagged or contain things like in-line xBRL. Most media files (audio and video) are also considered unstructured data.

> In contrast, data that is processed is structured data. Consider a contract in a Word document. We would classify the document as unstructured. But someone, or even an AI or ML application, reads that document and tags specific phrases and amounts with business-agreed names and definitions, such as the mortgage rate and outstanding beginning balance. When attached to an identifier for the mortgage contract, these values become structured data.

Tools like Hadoop, MapReduce, and Spark promised to be able to crunch big data on commodity hardware and deliver the single "golden source" data storage solution promised since the early days of relational databases. Data warehouses (and data lakes) provide a significant benefit, enabling the distributed storage of large sets of unstructured and unrelated data while applying tools that can efficiently access that data and provide analysis at fractional technological costs. One can point to the internet itself as an example of the functionality and productivity of this new form of approaching data.

However, both of these stores can rapidly turn into a data swamp. A data swamp is when a lake or warehouse becomes unwieldy, data quality suffers, and it becomes unusable. The causes are varied, but in many cases, the success of a lake or warehouse results in its demise. It is successful for a particular solution, so more is added. Additional business domains sign on and begin to add in their data. As with anything that proliferates, data management becomes more difficult. Not all data gets tagged adequately with metadata—or the established metadata tagging available is inappropriate for the new datasets, but we leverage it as a stopgap. Business domains are not correctly identified and kept separate. Instead, we ignore language variety, and datasets are incorrectly assumed to be the same or comparable. Contextual variety is lost. As with any swamp, the warehouse or lake becomes cluttered and difficult to navigate.

Data marts and data lakehouses were innovations meant to try and combat these eventual problems, but in essence, they are smaller instances of the larger lakes and warehouses. Lakehouses merge structured and unstructured data, ostensibly trying to remain with a single domain, but without proper domain definition, fail at this. This failure is because the focus is on the technology aspect of delivering the solution versus recognizing the language realities that cause data clashes and classification issues.

Before any warehouse, lake, mart, or lakehouse diehard becomes too upset, we must recognize that these solutions all have excellent track records of success and significant benefits. There are definite spaces where each of these solutions is a perfect fit, especially when using a mix of the solution types to address the data management problems they solve best.

Yet, being technology-first solutions for a problem we are defining as primarily a sociolinguistic problem at its core, there will always be an aspect of each solution that misses the mark as long as data managers and the technology solutions they use do not include something more than a semantic-context pairing as the social tooling component.

Data Mesh

At the time of this book, in 2024, the newest kid on the block is the data mesh. Big data has run its life cycle of new hype to unmentionable, so data mesh has stood up to stand in its place.

Still, there are conflicting definitions of what data mesh is and isn't in the hype cycle. This inconsistent definition has been the subject of several panel and boardroom discussions in which I have participated across the global chief data officer community. Among those CDOs I speak with semiregularly, I think we have coalesced around a general agreement of data mesh, which likely diverges with others. But, regardless, I'll be using that description here.

The main questions are whether data mesh is a technology to be implemented (meaning software and hardware solutions you can purchase and implement) or if it is a theoretical framework for organizing your data. It is an evolving methodology that merges much of the learnings since the dawn of data storage and computing and shifts its focus to a hybrid technological and theoretical framework approach.

Admittedly that was a significant amount of buzzwordy two stepping. Let's look at what I see data mesh is versus what it is not.

Data mesh should not be about data democratization just because everyone should have access to all data (though not everyone agrees about this). I find increasing, though still limited, agreement that not all data needs to be available to everyone. Note that this is unrelated to the security and access rights of data for sensitive data like personally identifiable information (PII). In a much more general sense, this statement corresponds to Langefors' theories on information systems, such that "some data are only intelligible to restricted groups of people."[4]

Data mesh technology solutions come after the theoretical data design. What datasets/stores should be included in a mesh and what data within those sets should be shared and linked needs to be determined ahead of technology deployment. Simply data meshing everything together will merely result in a mess.

Data mesh turns back on the long-held desire and belief that all data can and should be centralized. There is not a concept of some overarching golden source. Zhamak Dehghani, in their *O'Reilly* book, *Data Mesh*, states that "Data mesh, at its core, is founded in decentralization and distribution of data responsibilities to people who are closest to the data."[4] Dehghani explains how data mesh is a change in approach and an alignment with domain-driven design (DDD), an influential systems design concept introduced in 2003 by Eric Evans.

"DDD defines a domain as 'a sphere of knowledge, influence, or activity.'"[5] The alignment of data mesh with DDD provides a potential opening to integrate applied pragmatics. DDD was a revolutionary concept, breaking traditional system architecture norms. As such, it would be difficult to be critical that it did not go far enough.

While most looking at data mesh have some conceptual idea of using this to contain domain-specific data stores and help link these disparate sources, there is still less recognition of defining specific Communities of Practice and analyzing the "domains" in that context. This lack of recognition is probably the biggest lost opportunity or missing piece in the approach to data mesh today. Consider that DDD incorporates a developing concept of CoP—a sphere of knowledge or activity. What is missing, then, are the aspects of shared processes and activities focused on a particular goal while producing knowledge and improving, all while maintaining a shared culture. The aspects of specialization and more robust implications to language, culture, and activities round out CoPs more than the idea of basic spheres of activity, influence or knowledge.

Further, Dehghani notes domain archetypes are similarly one-dimensional: source-aligned, aggregate, and consumer-aligned. No criticism is intended, as without the introduction of applied linguistics, one would not consider the complexities of interactions and language that would significantly enhance these "domain types."

Source domain approaches look at organizing based on the source of data, that is the business operations that create the original data product (i.e., the *speaker*). This approach aligns well with the theories behind tracing lineage and preserving provenance. Meanwhile, consumer-aligned approaches look to who is receiving the data and focus on the modeling and structure of data focused on them (i.e., the *listener*).

Aggregate domain approaches recognize that "there is never a one-to-one mapping between a core concept of a business and a source system at an enterprise scale … there might be a lot of source-aligned data that ultimately needs to be aggregated into a more aggregate form of a concept."[6] In our discussions on CoP, we have previously seen this construct run horizontally across an organization, such as risk, marketing, or sales.

Dehghani advises against creating and relying heavily upon aggregate domain data, however. In doing so, it highlights the issues facing data managers today that we have already discussed—the pull between different perspectives between different CoPs. He even identifies the core problem, though without the inclusion of an applied linguistic view:

> I strongly caution against creating ambitious aggregate domain
> data … that attempts to capture all facets of a particular concept

… and serve many organization-wide data users. Such aggregates can become too complex and unwieldy to manage, difficult to understand and use for any particular use case, and hard to keep up to date. In the past, Master Data Management has attempted to aggregate all facets of shared data assets in one place and in one model. This is a move back to single monolithic schema modeling that doesn't scale … resist the temptation of highly reusable and ambitious aggregates.[7]

In many ways, data mesh is the rapid evolution of thinking within the data community. It is more empowered without the old limitations of technology, and the growing recognition of existing bottlenecks and long existing barriers. Great innovation is happening, but much of it is re-inventing explanations of existing linguistic issues. Dehghani points out that there will not be a single source of truth. He also notes that there will be concepts that are *common* across different domains, and they need to be linked. However, those polysemes will still need to be modeled based on domain-specific attributes according to the bounded contexts of their domains.[8]

Much like our discussion on dogs, across different CoPs, these concepts are considered revolutionary within the data community—but have been the subject of decades of research within the applied and sociolinguistics disciplines.

Data mesh offers an exciting opportunity to meld with applied linguistics as a revolutionary methodology. But currently, it is held back by being technology-led, and still resting on the simplistic, subjective, and biased ways of defining *the business* and *domains*. Data still needs to be recognized as a stored and written language, and that it carries the same properties, challenges, and potential solutions as all written and stored language.

Data Capture

The amount of data needed to function within financial services is beyond the scope of a single company or organization to generate or research independently. As is the interconnected nature of the social system, brokers have to communicate with investment managers, investment managers with custodians, custodians with infrastructure systems, and so forth.

There is significant verbal communication between firms and individuals throughout the life cycle. Still, much data is going back and forth, being collected and distributed between different companies. Some of these may be data vendors or other third-party service firms who are specialists in a certain area and provide data feeds to others—from price and analytical data to corporate actions to ESG (environmental, social, governance) and unstructured data. There were surprisingly many faxes, emails, and secure PDF documents. Yes, I did say faxes.

Of course, this is more data than any organization could handle manually. As a result, since the days of the computer, ways to capture data and process it for storage have evolved. Extract, transform, and load (ETL) processes are the powerhouse of data capture and processing, even if AI and NLP tooling are gaining traction.

In a three-phase process, ETL begins with extraction. The data source, which may include more than one source, is identified. This phase is typically concerned with identifying the type of data, the format in which it exists, and the schema or data definitions for the data. Two language questions then follow. First, ensure you know what data you are looking for and properly define what you need. Second, is examining the source data and understanding the definition of that data from the perspective of that source.

The second is a critical step, as a data source may appear from a summary description to fit the data need, but the actual content does not fit the desired definition. For example, I may be interested in buying a house, so I want to find all sources for real estate home listings. A data source may purport to provide real estate listings; however, upon further examination, those listings may only be commercial properties or open lots, as opposed to residential houses.

Transformation involves several actions, from simple field name translation to data cleansing. In our real estate example, perhaps the data we are importing is provided in a column format, with the price in a column labeled "P." In our dataset, we have labeled that field "Price." so in the transformation rules, we must be sure to map "P" to "Price." A more complicated issue may be that all the prices are in different currencies, but we want them all in U.S. dollars. So, we apply a foreign exchange calculation to transform the foreign currency into USD. Or, the data source indicates the house types for "townhome," "single-family," and "multi-family" as numerical codes "1," "2," and "3," but we want to represent them all in our dataset as the actual descriptive names—so we transform a "1" to "townhome," a "2" to "single-family," and a "3" to "multi-family."

The data cleansing aspect of transformation typically involves fact-checking the source data for potential error resolution. The automatic setting of rules can remove data deemed bad or outside of certain tolerances or flag it for manual checking by a human before allowing it into the target dataset. Maybe we are only concerned with houses in New Jersey, but the dataset we are transforming contains homes from the entire United States. Anything not based in New Jersey, we would eliminate. Or perhaps two fields describe a home's number of levels or floors. We check to make sure the two fields are equal and flag anywhere the two fields disagree to check later to see why there is a discrepancy.

Finally, during loading, we store our transformed data in our destination—whether a simple flat file, spreadsheet, database, or data warehouse. While this sounds like the simplest part of the process, we want to include audit information like lineage, date, and provenance details. This way, any issues can be traced back if there are questions about the data. Data age is an additional vital measure to ensure the freshness of data and a potential trigger for any refresh process.

Data Quality Control

The basics of data quality control may begin in data capture but persist beyond the loading stage. We need to monitor data for accuracy and completeness continuously. The reliability of data depends on its proper maintenance. Some data may be reasonably consistent such that it, and its definition, does not change over time. However, even the most static data will likely change slowly or have some update. And expect other data to be under constant change.

Understanding all these dimensions is part of maintaining proper data quality. If there are no updates to certain data, it should identify as stale and require remediation. We should maintain an adequate history for data that changes. We should measure changes against the current and historical records.

Data quality programs typically fit under a larger data governance program (discussed later) to ensure proper funding and governance. We can use different technological tools to run rules against the data to flag where there may be errors or inconsistencies. While some of these things may lead to automatic resolution, experts must analyze the flagged errors and make corrections in most cases.

I may be making this sound much too easy. First, not all quality metrics have a universal use. Different types of data must be measured differently—such as a simple difference between more static versus less static data. Further, much data depends on other data—their quality becoming relative. The quality concerns differ between transactional, contractual, and accounting data.

Expertise in not just what the data is but how we may use it and what function again points to the need to view data quality through the lens of CoP.

Data Lineage and Tracking, Workflow

Coming out of data quality was the recognition that understanding where data comes from, how it has changed, and the destination of use are factors that we should consider. Resolving errors made in decision making due to bad data is not easy if the source of the bad data cannot be found and corrected.

Before metadata, if we uncovered an error, we required significant manual work to investigate the cause. Where the data came from would have to be identified, as the final data likely went through numerous transformations and processes, all of which may have introduced small variations that had later impacts. The first immediate source of error would probably be simply compounding a data issue further upstream instead of the primary source of any problem.

The concept of data lineage and tracking dependencies between different datasets and processes mainly followed the traditional system interaction and workflow diagraming with which technologists were familiar. Flowcharts and systems diagrams illustrate the workflow through which data flows went, and metadata is appended to data to identify the system from which it originated and potentially the points at which another system or process altered it.

Most of this began and persisted on a dataset or table-level basis instead of individual data elements. "While table-level lineage has been the norm for several years, when data engineers want to understand exactly why or how their pipelines break, they need more granularity. Field-level lineage helps teams zero in on the impact of specific code, operational, and data changes on downstream fields and reports."[9]

Data lineage goes hand in hand with data provenance. Data provenance is akin to a historical record, or an audit trail, while data lineage is about the actual flow and relationships between systems and processes that use the data. However, this remains a purely systemic view of the data. One needs to abstract to another level to understand what CoP uses that data for and for what purpose. While we may be able to track data transformation, it is also not entirely clear why that transformation occurs and what its impact on its meaning is.

Data Analysis

It would be incomplete not to cover data analytics in a discussion about data. For many, the whole reason for having and gathering data is to analyze it, discover new insights and trends, and make decisions quicker, better, and faster than the competition. Beyond just making an organization function, an organization sees data as a resource (insert your water/oil/mineral analogy here).

Data analytics uses mathematics and statistics to analyze datasets. Typically trained in computer science, data analysts will use SQL, R,

Python, and other tools to gather data and mine it for information that may not be readily apparent or discoverable. This gathering may be because data sits across different systems or systems focused on processing or transactions versus query functionality.

Data analysis can focus on several different perspectives, but all focus on providing an answer to some question. We can recognize traditional analysis easily in things like research. For example, we are gathering all the available information about rivers over 100 years and illustrating how they have changed over time, from water levels to erosion to pollution. The idea here is to report on historical trends and provide information about certain topics.

Why something occurred is another focus. Instead of just informing people about how rivers changed over those 100 years, we can add more data. Questions can be asked, such as why did pollution increase or decrease in certain rivers? Why did water levels increase or decrease over time, and what were the different factors?

Both approaches are useful for companies, such as examining their past performance or competitors, investigating a new business opportunity, or gauging their success or failure in certain ventures. But more and more, analytics is about predicting the future. Based on all these things from the historical record, we can create what-if scenarios and make statistical analyses on what could happen in the future.

Finally, based on this predictive analysis, we can add more data to develop possible actions based on those predictions. These analytics are part of our day-to-day macro and microeconomic modeling. Still, firms have also taken them up to provide advice and guidance on specific strategic questions they may have about their business, from parking lot sizes to deciding how much of a product to stock on the shelves.

Master Data Management and Governance

All the previous sections deal with parts of the data life cycle. Overarching these sits the discipline of data management and governance. Data management and governance is about putting in the proper controls, oversight, and organizational structure, alongside the technical architecture necessary to capture, organize, and use data for an organization.

Multiple models exist for data management and governance assessment, which provide a framework for setting up a data organization. Typically referred to as a *maturity model,* the framework includes assessment tools that can be used to identify the parts necessary for data management and governance and measure how mature an organization is with its needs around data management.

Irina Steenbeek captured the most prevalent models in a 2018 article[10] and listed DAMA, DCAM, CMMI, IBM, Stanford, and Gartner. She notes that the models differ on several points, from an area of focus (where some models may focus more on the process, others on pure data management, and some lean more toward governance or software) to how certain aspects are classified (data strategy as a separate function versus being a subdomain of governance).

The IBM, Stanford, and Gartner[‡‡] models, built and published through the late 2000s and early 2010s, have not appeared to survive independently much past 2020. Regardless, these models provide a foundation for understanding data management and governance issues alongside key themes for consideration. While a deep comparison and analysis of each model is beyond the scope of this book, an overview of the three primary models and where they came from is helpful.

DAMA—DMBOK2

DAMA,[§§] originally the Data Administration Management Association, dropped the "Administration" as data became more than just an administrative function and eventually turned to simply using the acronym under "DAMA International." Founded in 1980, a professional association of data professionals operates independent chapters. The *Data Management Body of Knowledge* book (DMBOK) was published in 2015 and is now in version 2 (DMBOK2) and sets to provide

---

[‡‡]Accessed August 31, 2023, https://blogs.gartner.com/andrew_white/files/2016/10/On_site_poster.pdf.
[§§]Accessed August 31, 2023, www.dama.org/cpages/home.

a "comprehensive view of the challenges, complexities, and value of effective data management."¶¶

The book provides a set of guiding principles, a framework, and a common vocabulary for data management professionals. While there is a certification course (at a cost) for individuals, there is no formal assessment tool besides the book and accompanying literature and references.

CMMI

Carnegie Mellon University's Software Engineering Institute (SEI) originally developed the Capability Maturity Model Integration (CMMI) in 1987. Primarily sponsored by the U.S. Office of the Secretary of Defense and the National Defense Industry Association, the original goal was software maturity assessment.[***]

CMMI eventually moved to a different CMU subsidiary, the CMMI Institute, which is now part of the Information Systems Audit and Control Association (ISACA). Regarding its origins, CMMI is a required assessment for many U.S. government contracts in software development.

The maturity levels focus on maturity through five levels, from initial poorly controlled processes (Level 1), identified but reactive processes (Level 2), proactive processes (Level 3), and measured and controlled processes (Level 4) to focus on optimization and process improvement (Level 5). From a data perspective, the model focuses more on data management and government processes than providing a specific framework for establishing and building a data organization. However, the structure of CMMI and its status as a well-established assessment model in use by the U.S. government led to the EDM Council approaching them with an early Data Management Maturity Model (DMM) in 2012.[†††]

¶¶Accessed August 31, 2023, https://technicspub.com/dmbok2/.

***Accessed August 31, 2023, https://en.wikipedia.org/wiki/Capability_Maturity_Model_Integration.

†††Accessed August 31, 2023, https://ndiastorage.blob.core.usgovcloudapi.net/ndia/2012/CMMI/W15226_Young.pdf.

EDM Council and SEI jointly developed a final model, which EDMC handed ownership to SEI to provide as an open-source tool. The collaboration lasted through 2013 until EDMC came out with its DCAM model.[‡‡‡] ISACA discontinued support for DMM in 2022.[§§§]

DCAM

The EDM Council initially rolled out the Data Management Capability Assessment Model[¶¶¶] (DCAM) in 2013. DCAM is both a framework and certification program offered by the EDM Council. I will disclose that I have some bias here, having participated in the early development of DCAM and being DCAM certificated. Currently, DCAM 3.0 supports a broad set of industries, diverging from the initial focus on financial services. The EDM Council also developed a cloud-specific framework called Cloud Data Management Capabilities (CDMC).

DCAM and DMM paralleled each other for many years, and there was some work toward keeping interoperability between the two models from a maturity assessment perspective. However, DCAM did enjoy a higher level of commitment regarding development and expansion. As of version 2.2, an assessment of 38 capabilities within eight core components covering:

Foundations—1.0 Data Strategy and Business Case and 2.0 Data Management Program and Funding

Execution—3.0 Business and Data Architecture, 4.0 Data and Technology Architecture, 5.0 Data Quality Management, 6.0 Data Governance

Collaboration—7.0 Data Control Environment

Application—8.0 Analytics Management

Overall, DCAM is positioned to be able to be used to create a business case to start a data management function, as a paid-for training

---

[‡‡‡]Accessed August 31, 2023, www.finextra.com/pressarticle/57632/edm-council-breaks-away-from-cmmi-institute-data-management-model.

[§§§]Accessed August 31, 2023, https://tdan.com/data-professional-introspective-capability-maturity-model-comparison/30607.

[¶¶¶]Accessed August 31, 2023, https://edmcouncil.org/frameworks/dcam/#resources-faqs.

and certification for data management professionals, to provide an assessment and benchmarking tool, set out a strategic roadmap, and to use as a compliance assessment for regulation or other audit purposes.

Summary

Data management and governance is a complex task that spans more than just picking the right technology and architecture. The task requires an organization to manage and control for the benefit of the entire organization, which, especially in today's environment, relies predominantly on using data to function.

Maturity and assessment models and frameworks are precious tools. Yet, at the same time, there is likely room for growth. While there is mention of business strategy and data domains, there is reliance on traditional data methodologies and existing organizational structures. There is little to no discussion toward defining a data domain— although the term is used authoritatively, just as in most data literature today. There is a bias toward shared and agreed terms and definitions. There is a focus on data meaning versus data definition without the context of formally defined CoP. We have seen that meaning, even with context, is usually insufficient when dealing with interactions between different CoPs.

With the significant emphasis placed on the need for data domains and authoritative sources, one would think that there would be more in all of these models in terms of their actual definitions. We would not need this book if a solution to this complicated space existed. These models, though, provide significant value, although there is always room for improvement. They are excellent foundations and are continually evolving. One hope is that in the next stage of evolution, as opposed to more technology or business process enhancements, some of the sociolinguistic tools are introduced from this book.

AI and Machine Learning

What Are AI, ML, LLM, and NLP?

There is great promise lurking behind the concepts of artificial intelligence (AI), machine learning (ML), large language models (LLM), and natural language processing (NLP), including their various spin-offs like deep learning. For every person touting these technologies' futuristic possibilities, there are two that stand up about the risks and dire consequences.

As with anything widely discussed and pervades modern culture and fiction, there tend to be misunderstandings about what certain technologies encompass and do. So, for our purposes, let's first give some basic definitions of what AI, ML, NLP, and LLMs are and what they are not. Again, this is not a book specifically on these topics, so it gives a broad brushstroke with which many specialists in the field may find issues. However, the goal is to understand the data implications of applying these technologies.

Machine learning (ML) is probably the most basic and may have misunderstandings. ML harkens back decades to the older terms of "business intelligence," "expert systems," and "management information systems." Those systems relied on creating business rules that created a decision tree for problem-solving. By feeding these systems more data, we can correct the rules using the erroneous data so that the decision system can perform simple analytical tasks. Today, ML is mostly considered a subdomain of artificial intelligence and focuses on creating algorithms where the computer uses examples and feedback to program itself instead of a programmer writing every possible if/then statement.

For example, it might be simple for a human to look at a picture and identify a flower. But the variety of types of flowers—shapes, sizes, colors, and so forth—presents so many possibilities that it would be vastly complex for a programmer to capture. Consider the differences between a lily, dandelion, tulip, rose, and iris.

Yet, create an algorithm that looks at different characteristics and then trains with examples of what are and what are not flowers and where those characteristics exist in both datasets. Initial data can include the answer—formally providing training. Later datasets can ask the program to provide an evaluation—and be told if it was wrong or right. Over time, given feedback on its success, the program will eventually learn to distinguish between a flower and what is not.

AI, in contrast, sits above ML in that instead of being trained to perform a specific task well, it attempts to perform more complex tasks and, in a way, mimic human intelligence. So, we have trained our ML to recognize flowers, but it cannot tell us if those flowers are on trees or shrubs, and what those things it classified as "not flowers" actually could be.

Imagine we have trained other ML systems to perform those specific tasks. A highly evolved AI could answer the question, "What is this a picture of?" by explaining the different flowers, other plants that do not have flowers, insects and animals that may be present, and even rocks or a pond.

Of course, AI still has significant limitations. Ask that same AI for the best path through the garden, and expect it to behave like an autonomous driving car AI, and you'll be disappointed.

Natural language processing (NLP) is pretty much what it sounds like. Formally, it is an interdisciplinary field combining linguistics and computer science. However, this is only a personal opinion; NLP appears to rest more heavily on the technology side of interrogating language, tending to use linguistic rules we can encode.

The business intelligence approach of writing code according to specific rules based on dictionaries dominates NLP's origins. ELIZA was a popular simulation of a psychotherapist that would use pattern matching and substitution rules to appear to be responding to and prompt the user with new questions. The program used a basic script and rules to match user input to the best prescripted response.

Rules-based NLP had limitations, as the system would need to add rules and refine the script constantly. Much was also based on Chomskyan concepts of grammar being a system of rules, where those rules will create the right combinations of words to convey the required meaning. The "transformational grammar" approach has a base in the theory that all grammar is somehow based on some universal grammar and, therefore, has a rules-based structure that is innate to its existence.

This approach required creating massive rules libraries, which would become increasingly complex and interrelated, interdependent and conflicting. Rules-based NLP also worked better in constraint contexts or domain-specific instances (i.e., homogeneous speech communities or CoP with clear rules around language and jargon use). Trying to apply rules-based NLP on a general basis—such as unstructured text from news feeds—was inaccurate, as context and semantic meaning could vary widely. Computationally, this would start to push against the processing limits of capabilities available in the 1980s and 1990s.

Statistical NLP would, in contrast, focus on taking the entirety of a text (*corpus* or *corpora*) and analyzing the entire piece. Still computational, statistical NLP focuses heavily on mathematical models. It takes language input and uses algorithms to determine probabilities to parse text and then further analyze. Certain understood phrases and words are tagged, evaluated, and then re-evaluated. Also, we can analyze text against other text to determine the frequency of phases or statements, inferring accuracy or truth.

Statistical NLP can be a powerful enabler. Spell and grammar checks in word processing programs are good examples of this application. With a dictionary for a specific language, your word processor can highlight and question your use of your or you're, they're or their, here or hear, and so forth. And know if you are using American English versus British English when spelling favor versus favour or using a c or z versus an s when organising or finalizing your manuscript.

Statistical NLP can also help predict the next word in a sequence (which is different from GPT, which generates whole text). Sentiment analysis reviews structured and unstructured data for recurring phrases or words that can provide a view into opinions about a specific product, statement, or idea. It can also help summarize large bodies of text by finding and scoring recurring themes.

Enter the LLM

In contrast to prior NLP ventures, LLMs enable the analysis of text and basic prediction and combine with AI tools to generate original text and reason about it. More traditional NLP still focuses on a specific context area, with the underlying learning data being that *corpora lingua* is the foundation. LLMs also are typically pretrained but with significantly larger datasets. LLMs still use statistics, sentiment analysis, tagging, parsing, and the tools that underpin statistical NLP.

LLM, though, are enabled by different technical architectures and neural networks and usually incorporate more self-learning and unsupervised learning than traditional, more purely statistical approaches. The real difference with LLM is a matter of scale. Much as deep learning is massively scaled ML, LLM scales on top of deep learning, whereas traditional NLP methods rest atop ML methods.

ChatGPT

Michio Kaku referred to AI chatbot platforms as "glorified tape recorders" that "takes snippets of what's on the web created by a human, splices them together and passes it off as if it created these things. And people are saying, 'Oh my God, it's a human, it's humanlike.' He did not discount, however, that tools like these would benefit society and increase productivity—but was lamenting the fear people had about them becoming some "super intelligence."[****]

We are familiar with the potential of a superintelligence from popular culture. The underrepresented, good and benevolent smarter-than-the-smartest humans are in stark contrast to their world-dominating, human extinction-seeking brethren. It is *Iron Man's* J.A.R.V.I.S., *Star War's* BB8, *Star Trek's* Data, Chappie, and *Big Hero 6* versus a tidal wave of HAL (*2001: A Space Odyssey*), VIKIs (*I Robot*), Matrixes, Ultrons (*Iron Man/ Avengers*), Cylons (*Battlestar Galactica*), Skynets, Borgs (*Star Trek*), Maria's double (*Metropolis*), AM (Harlan Ellison's "I Have No Mouth, and I Must Scream"), Proteus (the *Demon Seed*), *Screamers*, and *Eagle Eyes. WarGames*

[****]Accessed August 16, 2023, https://edition.cnn.com/2023/08/13/business/ai-quantum-computer-kaku/index.html.

only gave us hope as long as Matthew Broderick stayed up to date on his tic-tac-toe skills.

Science fiction has oft predicted modern technological advances decades ahead of the general imagination. Philip K. Dick imagined facial recognition systems, Isaac Asimov wrote of flatscreen TVs, and *Star Trek* envisioned mobile phones (the "communicator"). Robots were envisioned as far back as Homer's *Iliad.* However, Karel Čapek takes credit for the "modern" robot concept in *R.U.R.*, and rockets, spaceships, powered flight, and submarines have been topics of literature for decades, if not millennia, before they were considered potentially realistic.

As with any technology, the reality is somewhere in between the naysayers and the fanatics. From AI to NLP, the truth is that they exist now and have great promise, but they are not near any point of matching even the most reserved depictions of modern science fiction automation.

We need to explore the why? Satyen Sangani, CEO and cofounder of Alation said; "Every day, organizations are gathering information about customers, buyer behavior, supply, inventory management, sales, customer service, and so on. This is big data! Yet incomplete data is the number one reason why AI fails."[††††]

ChatGPT 4.0

ChatGPT is an AI style and stands for Chat Generative Pre-trained Transformer. Generally, this means that, based on the training set of data, the AI will try to generate text, transforming information it has to answer or respond to input.

I asked two questions to test the system in mid-2023 when ChatGPT 4.0 was released (and there was a significant amount of hype around it).

First, I asked, "How can Applied Linguistics help in data management?"

[††††]Accessed July 1, 2023, www.forbes.com/sites/forbestechcouncil/2021/05/10/why-ai-projects-are-failing-at-your-company/.

ChatGPT answered: As an AI language model, I cannot provide a personal opinion. However, Applied Linguistics can help in data management as it involves the scientific study of language use and communication. This field deals with practical applications of linguistic research, including language teaching, translation, language policy, and corpus linguistics. In terms of data management, Applied Linguistics can help in analyzing large volumes of text data and developing natural language processing tools to process and manage this data efficiently. It also provides insights into language use patterns, which can be useful for data profiling, data cleansing, and data classification. Additionally, Applied Linguistics can help in designing effective data visualization techniques that communicate complex information in a clear and accessible way.

Next, I asked, "Why can't Applied Linguistics be used for data management?"

ChatGPT answered: As an AI language model, I cannot provide personal opinions. However, from a technical perspective, applied linguistics is not specifically designed for data management. It primarily focuses on the practical application of linguistic theories and principles to real-world problems in language teaching, translation, and communication. While data management is an essential aspect of linguistics research, it requires specialized skills and tools such as database management systems, statistical analysis software, and data visualization platforms. Therefore, applied linguistics may not be the most suitable field for managing large datasets and complex data analysis tasks.

Sangani's answer to this incompleteness is data democratization, but as we've already explored, not all data is for everyone. But this is not to say he doesn't have a point. Access to all the data doesn't mean that the data is complete. As we have discussed, semantic meaning, context, bias, and inferences based on language differences, intent, and interpretation all lead to an incomplete understanding of our data.[‡‡‡‡]

[‡‡‡‡]This goes to some of my arguments made in regards to the 2008 financial crisis previously.

So, what is going on here? Yes, both questions I asked the chatbot were leading questions. This experiment highlights Kaku's observation that these AI chatbots spit back recorded information instead of doing any *real* human thinking. The answers directly contradict each other, particularly in saying that applied linguistics is or is not appropriate for large, complex datasets.

> But what about so-called *autonomous* cars? They must analyze vast amounts of incoming data to make decisions, from speed, staying in their lane, and reacting to unpredictable actions from other vehicles, people, or animals being in the way. The AI makes real-time decisions based on variable input.

The first issue is that these examples are false equivalencies. In the latter example, the special training of the AI within a very specific discipline is a means to perform specific functions. I am not discounting that this is a highly complex task taking massive amounts of information in real time, analyzing and reacting to it. But all that information is specifically tailored toward the goal of driving needs. The AI isn't considering the grocery list to purchase at the supermarket or the list of appointments at work once they arrive. In the former example, the AI states upfront that it cannot provide "personal opinion," which is a nice way for its programmers and creators to say that the AI cannot provide specific analysis of a subjective nature.

We should acknowledge that through linguistic tools for scoring language, it could be possible for an AI to analyze all existing text, give a quantitative analysis of existing references to linguistics use in data management, and provide a weighted answer of references for one answer over the other. This inventory of available references may emulate "reasoned analysis," but this is still not "reasoned analysis." All this scoring and analysis is akin to educated guessing by the computer based on the given data and the training it has received. Also to be considered are the introduction of potential biases inadvertently before or during and the realization that computers do not understand context themselves but only from the perspective of their trainers.

A 2019 study examined the importance of context in regard to NLP comprehension, using LLMs and long short-term memory (LSTM) networks. The researchers noted in their conclusions: When language occurs as an interaction between speakers and listeners, it is a form of social action (Austin 1975). Therefore, accounting for the conditions of language's generation is a necessary step of analysis if we are to truly understand language in its communicative aspects, in any setting. But, even if we accept that "context matters," it is often difficult to determine exactly when context matters, and how its importance varies between domains and media. While we cannot exhaustively reapply this framework to other domains, constructs, and contextual data, language researchers across disciplines can conduct their own context-based analyses and contribute to the general body of knowledge on how context impacts language understanding.[11]

Context becomes difficult even when dealing with a well-trained NLP encompassing a large corpus. Across domains, context changes—that is, its use and meaning and impact on the semantic meaning of words and sentences are highly variable. Further, context can be particular to an individual or subgroup within any domain, so within a specific CoP, contextual clues may not accurately reflect any clear utterance that diverges from the established statistical norm.

Significant in this analysis is that the researchers also included historical knowledge of the individual speakers that contributed to the base corpus. "[T]here is a growing consensus about the necessity to model language processing in a way that accounts for the encoding of both linguistic and contextual information (Cai et al. 2017; Hay, Nolan, and Drager 2006; Kapnoula and Samuel 2019; Munster and Knoeferle 2018; Sumner, Kim, King, and McGowan 2014)."[12] Beyond context, this introduces pragmatics' properties—although in a limited sense. The introduction of some pragmatic-based views improved results. But this is still limited and an emulation. For an AI to incorporate true pragmatics, the creators and trainers must be able to inventory and model every possible input a person could take into account while processing an utterance—from historical experience to nonverbal clues and the environment. We are unaware of all the variables that impact our interpretation of utterances. It is not possible to automate the unknown.

So, Where's the Problem?

With all these tools, why can't technology solve our data management problems? In combined use, they would appear to have all the pieces necessary to sweep away the mass of confusing data, definitional issues, and language inconsistencies.

Any data management guru will tell you that *garbage in, garbage out* (GIGO) is a data guiding light. Of course, if your data is *dirty*, it will be unusable and corrupt all your *good* data. But that is what data quality control systems are for, right? Simply implementing a data quality control system should fix those issues.

But how is that data going to become clean? Data governance and master data management will provide the rules and regulations for clean data. We can even apply AI and ML to the data capture processes to make this efficient and automated.

But who is writing those rules? Who is making the decision that they will use to evaluate the cleanliness of captured data? Who creates the labels, schemas, tags, or structures that any data storage solution will leverage?

The typical model is that technologists—qualified computer and data scientists—may work with *subject matter experts* to create the basic rules and structures. Then again, they may not—given a format specification from a vendor, those technologists may follow the preordained rules and provided definitions to insert into their systems and infrastructures.

An additional problem comes into play when dealing with data. Meaning in data (i.e., meaning in language) "only comes to be meaningful as a consequence of use and, consequently, context of use guides meaning construction (Evans and Green 2006, 211 ff)."[13] This simple concept presents significant problems for data management (not to mention AI) as we typically store data as individually defined data elements. We perceive how that data got there as a lineage problem, but it really is a CoP-defined contextual meaning problem.

Redefining GIGO

Is it really garbage in? In many cases, it is really good data in, garbage out. We may not understand how to use the data correctly. If the data source is from a different CoP, we must consider the nuances of a different language. Just throwing up one's hands and stating, "That data is bad," is an easy out.

Notwithstanding, there is a lot of bad data—whether it is inappropriate for use because of its source, the data quality is horrible, or otherwise. But one should also consider our assumptions about the data from a listener's perspective. What biases are in play in considering or not considering certain data as a source—and is there expertise present that can appropriately understand the data?

The meaning of any stored data exists not as an individual entity roaming free in a vacuum but is composed of the whole in which it was used and came into being. It is the context of use, the intent of the CoP in that use, and the interaction with any other CoP that may have altered the intended or inferred meaning.

Porto Requejo refers to Evans and Tyler again, and they argue that "pragmatic meaning, rather than coded meaning, is 'real' meaning (Evans and Green 2006, 216). Coded meaning, as seen, for instance, in dictionaries, is in most cases nothing more than an abstraction made from all the previous contexts where the word has been used before. And this is finally why we should conclude that context is what leads the process of meaning construction."[14]

The Technology—Linguistic Knowledge Gap

The fact is that having a linguistics background is not a prerequisite for anyone looking for a job in NLP, AI, ML, LLMs, or any of the associated fields. Having a computer science or data science-related education and background is generally a requirement. Additionally, classes in universities on these subjects—and I'm being very general here—typically pay passing reference to linguistics, focusing on a few key things like semantics and more on the computational linguistics side. Take a moment and look up job postings for jobs in these fields. Any references I provide here will be gone long before publication, given the demand for skilled computer and data scientists. Linguistics graduates need not apply.

As an analogy, the relationship between computational and applied linguistics is like exploring philosophy only through mathematical models. Yes, mathematics is beneficial for philosophy. But, at the core, a sound foundation of logic benefits a philosopher. That you can use math to provide a logical basis for any philosophical theory does not mean that philosophy is just some offshoot of mathematics.

We can see this nuance in basic misunderstandings about language and linguistic tools, as in the following statement in an AI article in 2022:

"Why should you care about data semantics?
Data semantics is a deep technical concept.
But there's a single key takeaway you need to know:
– The Primary Concern of Semantics Is to Give Context (And
    Therefore Meaning) to Something –"§§§§

This conclusion is simply incorrect and unsupported by a vast amount of literature. The primary concern of semantics is to give meaning to a *word, phrase, sentence, or text.* Semantics does not *provide context.* Semantics is about meaning. Context influences semantic meaning. This difference is an important nuance influencing how someone may analyze text and create NLP systems.

Maria Dolores Porto Requejo of the Universidad de Alcala says, "From a Cognitive Linguistics approach, I will claim that context is not some extra information we turn to when bare semantics is not

---

§§§§Accessed August 17, 2023, https://aimagazine.com/articles/semantic-data-platforms-how-ai-gives-context-to-your-data.

enough. On the contrary, in real uses, context always comes first, that is, before the linguistic unit can be interpreted there is a big amount of information available to participants that will direct the process of meaning construction and determine which sense, from all the possible ones, must be selected."[15]

Nouraldeen states this another way, "Meaning and context are interdependent, that is, meaning cannot be communicated without context, and context cannot be established without meaning" and "To summarize, looking at words alone can lead to ambiguity, but context can provide critical information to identify the correct meaning."[16] Semantics does not lead to context.

Context does not provide all the answers for determining the correct semantic meaning. The goal or purpose of a context has influence. That is, the pragmatics surrounding any text include the broader view of the speaker, their knowledge of the listener, the listener, intent, inference, assumption, and potential disconnects during the communication.

Telling the Data Story

The *Data Story* has emerged as *data storytellers* explain that the reason people don't *get* data is because it is boring, too complex, or spoken about in technical terms that do not resonate with business-minded counterparts. Available visualization dashboards are sometimes too complex or difficult to interpret at first. But, perhaps one of the reasons for this difficulty is the lack of alignment in language. If the data is relevant to you, why do you need a story to make it relevant or understandable?

Data must have an important meaning for potential users to understand and can improve their decision making to make it to those users in a way they can act on it. However, a "recent study by the analytics database company Exasol showed that dashboards are still the most common tool for sharing data insights. However, 53 percent of the respondents agreed that dashboards are often overlooked since they are so time-consuming and difficult to interpret."[17]

There is a definite need to find clarity in communicating the message data is telling. Especially when the data may be complex or the underlying meaning is not readily apparent. Some intended audiences may understand the meaning but have difficulties retelling and expressing that meaning to others.

Creating an engaging and informative narrative allows for better retention of the information the data provides and the ability for others to retell and spread the information more effectively. Without an engaging story, potential users may be overwhelmed by the data, especially if they are not experts in data analysis. Further, stories have been what humans have used as a means to convey messages since before written language. Stories are one of the most effective means of communicating.

The academic world does not lose the importance of this skill. MIT's Sloan School has a Communications and Data Storytelling course as part of its Master of Business Analytics curriculum and Executive Education offering.[¶¶¶¶] Northeastern has an interdisciplinary Data Storytelling, Visualization, and Communication initiative.[*****] The University of Chicago, Stanford, Purdue, and Carnegie Mellon have online or curriculum courses in telling the data story.

An old adage says, "Let the data tell the story." But, for most people, just seeing information doesn't mean they process, remember, or realize its impact. People actively ignore information in many cases—some of which can be related to biases like confirmation bias or expertise bias, especially when information doesn't match their beliefs or expectations. Visualizations have helped somewhat, but many charts and infographics take effort for the reader to interpret and understand what they mean to convey.

By telling a story, people become more connected to what the data is saying. Tying the data to the real world—to people they care about, issues that impact them—makes them more invested in what is happening, just like any good novel or movie engrosses the individual or group. Stories are more engaging and memorable than just listing facts and figures independently.

[¶¶¶¶]Accessed November 3, 2023, https://executive.mit.edu/course/communicating-data-through-storytelling/a054v00000jk27LAAQ.html.

[*****]Accessed November 3, 2023, https://camd.northeastern.edu/research-scholarship-creative-practice/data-storytelling-visualization-and-communication/.

Further, telling a tailored story to a particular audience can help engage a group that is otherwise not engaged or doesn't see a connection to their needs. Imagine a firm hiring a third party to outsource parts of their noncore operations. The third party requests the firm to provide some additional information, but because it will be inconvenient to the firm, there is resistance. In addition, the question at the firm is, "Isn't that why we hired the third party in the first place?" Now, imagine the third party can illustrate a story with data showing that the firm providing the needed information will create significant positives over what the third party expects to deliver. One would think that the firm would change its mind and provide the requested information.

But that is not how it usually goes. One method is usually just stating facts—if you give us x, we can provide y plus x. This fact states the benefit, but it's just facts, and facts can be ignored or discounted without significant backup. However, just providing the data as proof will typically be waved away—no one wants to sift through reams of data to validate someone else's opinion. So, instead, the third party provides charts, shows sales impacts, customer wins, and all sorts of positive results. Again, the audience must focus on something they don't think they need to provide and that the third party is probably just trying to get away with not doing it themselves.

But an engaging story—perhaps how together they can find these untapped customers, help them, show them how the firm is essential to their lives, and how collaboration enables the firm to prosper, showing through visuals the before and after results that tie to the firm's core culture and mission—that may be the thing that pulls in the naysaying executives.

Bringing along an audience on a shared journey can have much more impact than just asking—or telling—them what to do or how to do it. But of course, this takes particular skills. First, the data must be sound and relevant. The storyteller must understand their audience and what drives them. They need to know what visuals will be easily consumed, explainable, and make the most impact. And the story itself needs to be logical, engaging, to the point, and concise. "Data storytelling is the skill to craft the narrative by leveraging data, which is then contextualized, and finally presented to an audience. It utilizes not only data analysis and statistics, but also data visualization, qualitative and contextual analysis, and presentation."†††††

The skills are not simple, and storytelling often conflicts with their more technical, logical aptitude when looking at data scientists, computer scientists, or quantitative analysts. Many may not even understand the need, referring to the adage that the data should show the logic without making up some story to convince someone of its integrity. Yet, expecting others to craft stories based on their analytical results leaves the possibility that the storyteller doesn't interpret or convey the information correctly, especially if they are not experts in the provided data. Tom Davenport, a prolific author and thinker in the world of data, states this purely as "Despite these compelling reasons for the importance of stories, most quantitative analysts are not very good at creating or telling them."[19]

As noted, there are significant academic resources dedicated to data storytelling. There is also a large body of books devoted to the subject. Almost all of them highlight the importance of understanding the storyteller's audience and contextualizing the data and story to fit the audience. The same data might be relevant to a salesperson and a risk manager, but they will have different views and perspectives on what is important and what insights the data should mean to be relevant for them.

Yet, at the same time, data storytelling is positioned to simplify complex topics and convey them to a broad audience. "Data storytelling is the process of transforming data analyses into an understandable storyline for a wider audience in order to influence the decisions of business users and other stakeholders."‡‡‡‡‡

At this point, we can state that data storytelling is essential and challenging—especially for more technically minded data people, and requires interpretation, audience awareness, understanding of the data, inclusion of context, and creation of a compelling narrative. It is hard

---

†††††Accessed August 9, 2023, www.thoughtspot.com/data-trends/best-practices/data-storytelling.

‡‡‡‡‡Accessed August 9, 2023, www.jaspersoft.com/articles/what-is-data-storytelling.

to argue about cultivating skill and activity to help rationalize and democratize the insights that data should bring to key decision makers and influencers.

But, given the key themes in this book that revolve around CoP, how semantics and context are lacking in the complex understanding of data, issues around bias and context, and lack of knowledge around pragmatics, there should be some concerns about data storytelling. Who is creating the story? Who is telling it? And to whom are they telling the story? And for what purpose?

Are data storytellers linking the right data with the right audience? Or do they create any connection—however tenuous—between the data and the intended audience to highlight the importance of data in general? One can imagine that any bit of data, however esoteric, put in the right frame or story would seem highly relevant and important. But this doesn't mean it should be a priority or has any immediate impact or relation to the target audience's primary goals and needs.

Is the storyteller contextualizing the data, introducing a bias to fit their audience instead of ensuring that the data natively has relevance to a certain audience and needs to be explained in context? Storytelling can take on a life of its own. Does the storyteller already have a bias toward the story they want to tell? Do they understand the data and appreciate their expertise, biases, and CoP? Do they have expertise in the CoP that their audience belongs to? And if they are generalizing to reach as broad an audience as possible, what are the implications of those nuances we leave out?

Much of the academic and professional literature suggests that the issue of bias is a key consideration in crafting any story. Yet, there is the counterforce of the story's goal being to convince others of a particular viewpoint. Even with data in hand, if a story is not making the desired impact, there can be the human tendency to pivot or slightly adjust the story to be more engaging and convincing.

If the storyteller isn't an expert or a member of the target audience's CoP, they could inadvertently drift from the true meaning of the data to make a connection with their story. Data storytellers from a data world that uses just semantic meaning and context may not fully appreciate or address the pragmatic issues in creating a story.

Regardless, in the end, it depends upon the data. And if the data is unaware of a Community of Practice, then the storyteller will likely not, either. The lack of awareness makes it much easier for the introduction of biases.

Do We Have Data Stewards Wrong?

Suppose the essence of pragmatics is to understand the interaction between speaker and listener, including the surrounding context, environment, history of interaction, and purpose. Why would we manage meaning within the confines of a single-user community?

Data stewards are a formal part of data governance programs today. They are typically business people who liaise between the technology organization and their business area concerning data usage. While this includes data security and access, one typical role is also managing the metadata surrounding the data they "own." This structure will usually follow the same domain-driven design concepts discussed previously regarding data mesh.

But, the focus on the data steward is mainly inward. Even an enterprise-level data steward will be concerned about their individual CoP—the *enterprise* view of data. As we have explored, how an organization defines and understands its data can vastly differ from the definitions belonging to individual CoPs that aggregate into the "enterprise view." In consuming information from outside their domain, the data steward will seek to (hopefully) transform that data into the language and definitions of their own CoP. Of course, suppose they do not appreciate the inherent language differences that exist between their CoP and those that they are sourcing data from, and do not transform it. In that case, immediate data quality problems are likely to occur.

However, we rarely ask whether the individual or group acting as a data steward has the expertise and knowledge outside their CoP. Do they have the cross-CoP bilingualism necessary to understand the speaker in context and provide a more robust and complete translation?

We can exemplify the value of this cross-language expertise with some entertaining examples of rote language translation, especially when we translate signs in Mandarin and other languages to English. There are numerous picture examples of a fire extinguisher with an English translation of the sign saying "hand grenade."

> "This was a Chinese translation without context. '火' means 'extinguish' or 'destroy,' '灭' means 'fire,' and '瓶' means 'bottle.' The original mistake appears to have been that the translator misinterpreted an item that is used to create fire with one that extinguishes it. Hence he/ or she must have settled on a grenade."[§§§§§]

At a buffet, the sign noted that the food was "Paul is Dead."

> "The Arabic word 'بولميت' is 'meat ball,' so this must have been a direct transliteration of our favorite spaghetti sauce. The error may have cropped up when 'بولميت' was translated back into English. More specifically, 'ميت' could also mean 'dead.' Similarly, given the way Arabic script deals with 'p,' 'بول' could also be translated into English as 'Paul.'"[¶¶¶¶¶]

Of course, this doesn't only go one way and isn't limited to small oddities. Global corporations are susceptible too. When it expanded in China, KFC had its "Finger Lickin' Good" slogan directly translated into Mandarin. Unfortunately, the translator ended up promoting "Eat Your Fingers Off."[******]

The examples you can find online by searching "language translation fails" can occupy someone for a full day. But a recurring theme reveals itself—lack of contextual knowledge and awareness of the listener's environment. So, when sourcing data from outside your CoP, are you

---

[§§§§§]Accessed August 28, 2023, https://scrybs.com/blog/humorous-machine-translation-fails/.
[¶¶¶¶¶]Ibid.
[******]Accessed August 28, 2023, www.mashed.com/747566/the-hilarious-translation-mistake-kfc-china-made-with-its-slogan/.

relying on documentation and translation tools to give you the right answers? There is more value in having someone who has "been there, done that" and understands the data and the context from both the speaker's and the listener's perspectives.

In that same path, there is a need not just for tagging but also for creating a metadata structure around data, sets of data, and messages containing data. It is critical to be able to identify not just the source but the context of the creation of source data, how that translates into the context and needs of the destination CoP, and the created discrepancies between the original data and the resulting information that is stored and recreated.

My Taxonomy Is Not Your Taxonomy—And That's Alright!

Taxonomies are a way to classify things in a way that keeps all related things together in a neat parent-child association. They're hierarchical by nature—each fork of a parent inherits the parent's qualities and adds new potential properties. They are beneficial for organizing items in a way that makes it easier to group data about them. Take cars—the parent being *types of transportation*—for example. Types of transport could be water vehicles, air vehicles, space vehicles, and road vehicles. Under road, we can have cars, trucks, and motorcycles. Then, under cars, we can have SUVs, sedans, muscle cars, and so on.

Of course, taxonomies are somewhat rigid, and once you have created a structure, adding to that structure can be challenging. Such a challenge would be exceptions like a water plane or duck boat. These both cross the established groupings—so which tree do you classify them under? Or do you make a new one? Taxonomies can also be duplicative. Imagine inserting a *hybrid* property or category into an established taxonomy. Do judgment calls have to be made about what belongs where—such as what was meant by trucks? Does that include the F250, or just things bigger than a boxcar?

Digital assets are the newcomers to the financial services world and have drawn interest. But what is a digital asset? Is it a cryptocurrency like Bitcoin or Ethereum? What should be considered a cryptocurrency? Should Central Bank Digital Coins (CBDC) be considered cryptocurrency? What about stablecoins? Are stablecoins CBDC? What if a "real world" asset is "tokenized"? Or is a debt instrument only issued on-chain? Are nonfungible tokens (NFTs) digital assets? What if the NFT is for a piece of artwork or a World of Warcraft sword?

In an ongoing working group effort with standards experts from multiple national and international industry and standards organizations, at least five taxonomies define what a digital asset is (and isn't) and the classification hierarchy that applies. Of course, each taxonomy is different. This difference begs the question—shouldn't they be the same? Why can't we have one taxonomy everyone uses and agrees to? They're all digital assets, aren't they?

Well, as it turns out, it depends. And typically, the common denominator is the CoP that supports one taxonomy over another. As seen with types of transportation, taxonomies are hierarchical and tend to cast as wide a net as possible. The trouble is that different CoPs often have different taxonomy views for the same *thing*. For example, some consider a convertible bond an equity, others as fixed income. Conversely, some treat preferred equity as fixed income versus equity. And we can consider that there would be different taxonomies for dogs based on CoP.

Hierarchies are very rigid and static. As Mike Dillinger, PhD, puts it, "Today's taxonomies rely to a great extent on long-standing, traditional assumptions and simplifications that come from formal logic. For example, the radically simplifying assumptions that any item can have only one parent and that all items have to be accounted for means that by design we can't represent the hybrid, ambiguous, or unknown items that populate so much of the world in our brittle, rigid categories".[††††††] They do not lend themselves to multiple views, perspectives, or messy matrix approaches. They do have their uses, however. Taxonomies, when applied within a specific CoP for a particular use case, can illustrate the specific meaning and relationships from that specific perspective

---

[††††††]Accessed January 18, 2024, www.linkedin.com/pulse/better-taxonomies-knowledge-graphs-mike-dillinger-phd-jdjoe/.

and help definite association in the language of the CoP using such a taxonomy.

A specific taxonomy can also highlight what is important to any particular perspective. With digital assets, taxonomies vary because certain hierarchies may be more relevant for one CoP over another. Some differentiate between currency-like assets versus digital assets based on more traditional products like bonds. Others look at the hash (the digital fingerprint) and the underlying technology platform. Another taxonomy only looks at currency-like assets but differentiates its hierarchy based on funding models and underlying associations such as fiat currency or deposits.

Tying these different taxonomies together, however, is a challenge. With different parent-child relationships, each taxonomy appears as a different skeleton—not as a variation of the same creature, but as different animals entirely. We saw this dichotomy in the discussion on dogs previously. How one community may need to classify and sort data associated with the same concept may vary widely. However, this is not wrong, as it fulfills a need for that specific community.

Confusion begins when we model something and build it out as we add more information and complexity. We focus on putting all the information and data into one big happy picture, which ends up very messy and conflicts with itself.

So, the challenge first is understanding what you are trying to model, why, and for what audience. Then, finding where you'll be getting your data, how those sources view their data, and how they may have different definitions/views/purposes for that data usage would potentially mean that data, natively, may not be an exact match for your needs.

CHAPTER 10

Pragmatics in Practice

So, I have beaten up on technology-related solutions and their approach to AI and NLP. The overreliance on semantics and the mathematical solutions from computational linguistics that neatly align with computer programming methodologies has not solved higher-level context and cross-domain communication issues. Merging disparate datasets is still messy, although experts will point to self-learning LLMs that eventually perform better and better at these tasks. I've put data storytelling to task as insufficient and potentially misleading while acknowledging the value it does bring.

I've complained that there is no concept of a speech community, or Communities of Practice, in current data practices. We speak about domains in broad brushstrokes of industry or function like financial services or self-driving cars but without any specific methodology. Standards creators huddle around in small like-minded groups and weed out dissenting opinions in pursuit of consensus creations that don't offend anyone—or ignore those that may be different.

Yet, I don't want any of this to be seen as me yelling, "You're all doing this wrong!" That would be hubris and not my intention at all. As data practitioners, we have come so far in such a very short time. Technology has advanced on Moore's law, and the tools and systems available have opened up so many new possibilities that technology is no longer a gating factor but a massive enabler to solving untouchable problems. The opportunities open to data professionals are seemingly endless and still open to the imagination.

As with any change, however, there is a risk of not evolving and instead trying to solve old problems with the same thinking, albeit with shiny new toys. Moving a spreadsheet into a database may seem like a step forward. Still, it doesn't solve anything if columns aren't defined, and your process for sharing and updating the data still involves an individual manually going into the database.

What we miss is remaking how we view data and *domains* (more formally, the definition of language communities through CoP), and instead of trying to force an overarching ontology across all of them, looking to create multiple ontologies that are more focused and specific to each community. Then, we can see how these different ontologies need to interact with each other (e.g., the use cases that cross over from one CoP to another). We can identify what requires language translation from one ontological definition to another, replete with the metadata changes that must occur from one nuanced definition to another (and necessarily change the nature of that data in the process).

This kind of approach, though, does not fit the common current modes of development. One of the primary drivers in technology development is cost savings—and the reuse of existing infrastructure and solutions is a key part of that thought process. Proof of concepts are used as agile ways to fail fast or prove a successful path. This results in data projects and standardization efforts that try to create an ontology in one domain as a proof of concept, then expend tremendous energy attempting to extend that same ontology. We can instead look at how we create multiple ontologies independently and then stitch them together based on the use case and meaning under the guidance of a pragmatic view.

Let's Not Shift the Paradigm

As mentioned, I do not advocate throwing out everything and starting from scratch. For years, technology limitations restricted our focus on data. Compute power limitations forced us for years to hold only two characters for a date year. Tapes could only store so much data, and the focus of data centers was on a library inventory system to find stored information. The introduction of the desktop PC fragmented the data-sharing ecosystem. As the ability to store information increased rapidly, we lacked the techniques to organize it in traditional normal-form tables. Documentation exists—but in, well, documents. We must manually comb through Word and PDF files to decode databases created decades ago or last year.

In 10 years, we have created data governance and management foundations. Compute power and storage are relatively cheap and easy to access. More advanced data analysis-focused programming languages and models, such as R, Python, RDF/OWL, Web Ontology Language, knowledge graphs, and more, have been created. Methods for tagging unstructured data and processing natural language through bags of words and predictive reasoning have massively increased capabilities.

Yet, consider this basic everyday occurrence. I have two systems that I want to connect, as one produces output that the other system needs, and today, we handle this by reports generated from the first system and data input into the second system. I want to map the data in the databases so that when an action occurs in the first system that should flow downstream, it triggers an update in the second system.

Today, I have to gather business experts from both processes. And business analysis that can write business and functional requirements. Each group have complete documentation on data definitions within their databases. We look at the data in the first system's database and compare the fields to the reports to find that the labels don't match the first or even the second system's database. Someone suggests that if both systems must interact, all the data should be migrated and harmonized to a single data store. We spin up the cloud space, and after an hour of discussing without resolution on whose price field we should use, we schedule another meeting. Technologists suggest they can store both fields next to each other. But code exceptions have to be written depending on which process is running.

And this doesn't include ancillary systems that each group may use —or possible other dependencies on other groups and systems that may be related. The second system's users are likely just a part of a larger functional group that performs other work. Following the documented middleware as a blueprint will rewrite what is already in place. Suddenly, this simple-looking project becomes unwieldy. But the answer comes down to throwing more programmers at the problem to sort out the things that fall through the cracks in the first rollout.

Even exploring data mesh, the approaches revolve around supporting domains. But domains remain undefined. There is also little guidance on creating interoperability between these data islands that contain subjectively classified domains. There is still much to evolve regarding how these domains interact in multiple fashions—as one single model can't represent all domains, and domains are messy, overlapping, and duplicative.

Imagine, instead, that we have formally defined CoP so that it is clear what systems, processes, inputs, outputs, and personnel share a common function, language, and data definitions—not decreed by organizational structures or conveniences. Where two CoPs intersect, we use data lineage to document what transforms and how they move from one function to another. We do not do this according to systems, physical infrastructure, architecture, or personnel reporting lines.

The problem is no longer an exercise in gaining agreement on whose concept of price is correct or preserving two different price fields and coding based on the use case. The focus is on who the CoP is accessing and using the data and how the transformation should meet their specific concepts and meanings that align with their language, processes, and functions. It is a shift in how we approach the problem from an analysis and process perspective instead of creating a new system development life cycle. The "business" is not looked at as one monolithic thing or a group of silos that we need to break. Individual CoPs have goals and objectives that have specific purposes, and the goal of data and technology should be to enable those individual CoP goals in light of the interdependence with other CoPs that have different goals and objectives.

Take the DCAM pillar of identifying domains. This one part is undeveloped and needs to undergo an evolution that recognizes CoP, not technology systems, individual use cases and processes, as driving data definition and use. The start is the amorphous concept we keep referring to in the industry as "domains." What is a domain? What constitutes a domain? Does what one individual conceives as a domain match what others believe is the scope of a domain? Perhaps this is a place to start.

First Things First

We do not formally define *domains*. We use loose terms that we assume knowledgeable people agree with. In financial services, everyone refers to the *front office* and generally accepts what this encompasses and means. However, some may consider the front office traders, not sales. Some may assume to combine fixed income and equity front office, while others consider these different. Is the front office without differentiation between buyers and sellers—that is, between investment managers and broker-dealers? The potential for disagreement on the actual definition of a simple concept reveals what could be fairly significant differences in how data is defined and used. The commonality of language due to shared specific processes, shared function (use cases), and culture become those defining lines.

At the same time, we need to remember that these are multidimensional models. We need to note that they will create overlapping Venn diagrams of CoP (e.g., *front office* shares many commonalities versus the *middle office* or *back office*, while *equity* slices across all three of those). Today, even when data managers organize by *domain*, it is based upon these rudimentary and personal or environmental factors that define what is considered the *domain*. If one group has created a dataset around the *front office*, and two others have created datasets specifically around *equity* and *fixed income*, these will not necessarily be immediately compatible.

But, this is less an issue than at first look—because this conveniently also illustrates the intersection points between specific communities where language (data) translation needs to happen and where we make single taxonomies, ontologies, and standards for those specific communities in relative isolation. Then, that translation between *shared data* can be done. Because shared data is uncommon, while shared in different contexts, for different purposes, and with different semantic meanings. While it passes from one community to another, necessary changes are made to that data to bring it into a new context. Wrapping this all together is the definition of a pragmatic view of that data.

There is a growing awareness of the importance of context. Yet, the data community has to consider why context differs, aside from user preference or a general feeling of "that is how that group does it." Rightly, there is a focus on when data is shared and where errors occur—and this is where we expend much effort in trying to *fix* the data so that it is compatible with both sides of the equation.

The action can either take the form of plugging holes in the dike one at a time until one runs out of fingers or wholesale re-architecture projects that attempt to model two different systems or groups that interact into a single dataset, system, or process while creating context labels to account for data inconsistencies. Both of these approaches are suboptimal. In the first case, it's a constant fire drill, finding each data point that needs translating and potentially causing more inconsistencies. In the latter case, there is an aspect of boiling an ocean without considering the different temperatures the creatures need to survive.

There is a bit of an onion to peel. One of the challenges today is how most individuals, regardless of whether they are in data, technology, or "the business," think about the world around them based on their personal feelings and experiences, further influenced by the formal structures a company they work for has organized itself. Companies taking a functional structure in creating their available units still have followed the biases of individuals (as senior and experienced as they may be) in what should be considered in-group or out-group for any particular "function." "Matrix" organizations have acknowledged the interdependence between different groups but still assign specific responsibilities to one group or another, and those groups are still defined subjectively. There are even instances of multidisciplinary flat organizations that throw all the different subject matter experts together to aim at a specific goal (think of the previous skyscraper building example).

Seasoned industry professionals responsible for creating organizational structures "know" their industry and the different components that make it up. Yet, a significant portion of subjectivity still comes into play when they do so. Based on many factors, the "front office" conceptual idea will vary from one professional to the next. This variance is less of an issue when discussing the process in broad brushstrokes. But when trying to apply data and technology solutions, the nuances between the needs of a syndicate desk and those of a secondary market trade support group do matter.

Subjectivity propagates into systems and data, in how we organize the technology and data organizations, and systems are built and managed. Subjective separations from one company to the next may make logical sense, say either separating sales and trading or not. However, these are still subjective decisions based on some processes we may or may not document. They may be logical decisions, but the basis is on the feelings and experiences of whichever individual is in a position of authority.

But what are the alternatives?

Should one global standard be created that forces a clear and precise definition of a "front office" in the financial industry? This definition would mirror the problems of creating a single common language across the financial services industry. What about the differences between a small firm and a larger firm where combining or separating functions would be more logical or where a firm may wish to outsource execution or trade support? There also may be legal definitions or restrictions across different jurisdictions that enforce the separation of certain functions based on individual market needs or concerns.

So, should regulators for a particular jurisdiction be prescriptive and define each part of the industry they jointly regulate? This point again runs into issues where the focus of regulation is rightly more on the performance of a particular function and why, as opposed to how the individual or firm is defined or classified. Indeed, regulations sometimes require an entity performing a particular function to register in a particular role—which speaks to function and action coming before role definition. Further, there are ongoing efforts in the standards world that both include and do not include regulators that struggle to find common ground in attempting to create commonality regarding data definitions.

In any case—both of these approaches would still be subjective, diluted by issues of generalization, biased by unintentional exclusion of differing perspectives and experiences, or by the dominance of certain authorities. Ultimately, these efforts either become too rigid for innovation and development or too general to be useful. They then lose sight of the goal of better understanding and managing data and continue to struggle with cracking the data code.

Let us start with the premise that the current method—some subject matter expert with some authority making subjective decisions about organizational structure—is not necessarily wrong or bad. The issue is that there is no persistent methodology to the decision making that can be repeated, nor is the understanding of the subjective logic captured formally or shared with those managing the data. There is also no feedback mechanism for controlling the model as it evolves due to all the potential factors, from company growth, competition, and market evolution to acquisitions, regulatory change, and new product innovations.

We force data managers to contend with an organization structured on the informal understanding of some individual or group's perception of the social system within that organization to perform its function(s) and the subsequent natural evolution of that social system over time. So, the data manager's most obvious option is to model the data along the formal organizational structures that exist or according to the specific systems that support those structures. This modeling is how they include context and work through semantic tooling to resolve data inconsistencies.

However, what if a data manager first surveyed the organization through a CoP lens? In doing so, do they gain an understanding of language, culture, and purpose differences regardless of defined organizational structure and systems? Maybe this is too large of a task for complex organizations and is likely overkill for small organizations. But, consider taking this first defining activity when starting any new project.

Ask if the project dimensions involve one or more CoPs. Is the project goal supporting the goals of individual CoPs, a larger social system, or both? Where is data—and language—shared versus not shared? Where are definitions different, or have different interpretations, meanings, or implications?

At this point, investigating the pragmatic interactions between CoPs can offer new insight into potential data reorganization. There will be a need to identify CoPs not involved directly in the project's scope—specifically where dependent data enters or leaves the bounded scope of the processes involved. But there is no immediate need to try and capture an organization's entire existing social system—just creating an initial foundation.

Yes, There Will Be Changes

We do not want to upend the entire system development life cycle or the data management structures. These are currently well-developed and, in most cases, work efficiently. We are looking for the evolution of these and other processes and how data managers and others think about how an organization functions.

Change is still required. As alluded to above, the key to cracking the data code is inserting the identification of CoP early in any data effort. Insertion should not replace or supplant existing steps but enhance and inform. As such, to have a process that consistently incorporates a CoP and pragmatics-based mindset should be one of the core foundational efforts undertaken.

While CoPs typically are viewed as informal communities, I offer that within an organization, one should be able to define domains of activity that share common practices, goals, and customs and the leverage of these activities to perform a particular function or set of functions. These are more than speech communities but are bounded by an organization's structure, allowing for applying a more formal scope to the CoP.

Identifying CoPs in an organization likely benefits most by focusing on "domains of interest." But, as we have asked before, what is a *domain*? Taking the last piece of what makes a CoP, namely a shared function or the performance of a set of functions, first, one method would be to use this to help bind and identify a CoP. To validate that this is a valid CoP, examining if the involved individuals share common practices, language, and culture would be necessary.

The Silo

One method to start defining CoPs can be to identify what are considered silos within an organization. Silos carry a negative connotation as being insular, inward-looking, and protective. Yet, otherwise, they embody much of what defines a CoP. Further, examining the reasons we may view silos as insular many times comes down to issues concerning language differences, intelligibility, and cultural differences.

But any group deemed a silo within an organization must also be performing a needed function that other areas have dependencies on, in which case there must be connections into and out of the group for the broader social system of the organization to function. By identifying a silo as a CoP, then, one can instead address the language and cultural barriers that impede better communication and interaction with other CoPs within the organization.

Instead of engaging a silo from the perspective that its members are doing something wrong, the question turns to understanding why they operate the way they do, how their language and data make the group perform better, and how the language is different from other communities. Enabling the silo to continue to perform how it functions—especially if it is successful—while simultaneously understanding how to better translate their data and language properly for more efficient and accurate use can better leverage that group's specific expertise and uncover where else it may apply.

Further, discovering their dependencies can enhance how data is translated into the group to increase data quality and availability, focusing on supporting the group's role and function. This discovery can only enhance learning, both within the "silo" as well as across the wider organization. Further, identifying a "silo" and encouraging a CoP perspective can encourage the "learning" aspect of CoPs, as opposed to simply being a task-based functional group of experts. Enabling a "silo" to exist by addressing language and cultural barriers and encouraging a learning environment focused on continual improvement not only enhances the group's effectiveness but its ability to service the larger social system of the organization as a whole.

In essence, we are looking not to break down the walls between silos, but making them more translucent, easier to see through but recognizing they are still there.

Discovering the Linkages

As CoPs are discovered, through identifying silos or other methods, a map should begin to appear of how those different CoPs are related to each other. Discovery can take many forms through process maps akin to assembly-line analysis, functional interactions, or dependencies. While in many cases, most individuals will identify as belonging to one particular CoP, there likely will be some crossover where individuals belong to two or more CoPs, especially with significant interaction or dependencies.

This discovery shouldn't muddy the picture but help enhance and illustrate where certain CoPs connect and interact and also begin to indicate why. Understanding the environment that two CoPs interact in and their dependencies is one step forward to taking a pragmatics-led view of how information in the form of data and language flows between those CoPs.

The more tightly coupled the two CoPs are, the more obvious it should be that they will share more similarities in data and language. For example, trade support, even if it is considered a separate CoP from trade execution for some organizations, will likely overlap. But as the circle widens, say to the middle office, there will naturally start to be more terms, data, and language that diverge. Further, the functions the community is performing and the purpose they are looking to achieve will differ. These should be clues to where we can draw boundary lines between communities. Even if they appear to use the same terms and definitions, one community (usually downstream on the trade execution flow) will likely translate data received from one community into the required form.

The differences in language change from one CoP to the next may appear very small when comparing one to the next in a communication chain. But now, if we pull back and compare the language between two ends in the chain—say between the syndicate desk and back office operations performing settlement functions for the secondary market—the gulf in language diversity becomes much clearer. Of course, these two CoPs typically never directly communicate, so one may ask why to worry about classifying their data and language by CoP. One of the most obvious answers would be data aggregation across an enterprise. Some communities span horizontally across vertical-focused communities and look at data from many different CoPs.

Remembering the study where organization leaders go with their guts to make decisions because they do not trust the data, this is one of the main struggles for data professionals. Data comes from multiple CoPs that speak different languages and use the same terms but have different definitions and meanings. The focus of enterprise data managers has always been to "normalize" that data. However, it is a messy task subject to data quality issues. Much of this is a result of the language disparities between CoPs. However, without identifying the source of the language disparities, data managers are left with top-down, ad hoc, or one-size-fits-all approaches that are not portable or scalable..

By creating a CoP map of an organization unbounded by shared systems or strictly viewed through an organizational structure, data managers can better understand where languages may be the same and where language differences exist. This understanding does not just identify semantic differences but contextual ones based on specific CoPs.

Integrating Pragmatics

So, why create another layered dimension on top of the existing system, organizational, process, and functional views? If we allow for data that CoP organizes, we have already conquered part of the problem of specialized language and data in context. Data stored by a specific CoP, in their definition and language, preserves the context and the interdependent semantic meaning of that data within the context of that particular use. Therefore, without even tagging these properties through metadata, there is at least an informal association between the data and its intended meaning in the proper context. The problem comes when this data needs to be shared or used outside of this CoP contextual boundary.

Individual groups are already functioning and handling language discrepancies mostly through experience. There is an argument that this may be "extra work" as experienced users are already translating, in their own minds, on the fly when need be. Pragmatics comes into play at this point when discussing the interaction between a speaker and listener—that is, the transfer of that data from one CoP to another CoP. Here, we can detail the environment, the semantic meaning both CoPs may have within their contexts, and the differences between those meanings regarding the data they share. Further, we are looking at the history and purpose of the interaction. The passing of the lineage of the data and the transformation of meaning over the process indicates points where semantic meaning changes—based on the CoP, the context, and the purpose.

The experienced user that has learned, over time, how to straddle the line between CoPs, understands where the differences in language and meaning exist and performs accommodation or repair functions on the fly, mitigating the data discrepancies in the systems when they share data. This is fine when you have those experienced users. But one should not forget, that they likely made many mistakes along the path of learning, and new users still need to learn, making their mistakes along the way as well.

Data managers can help by focusing on the key areas of discourse by first standardizing data models on either side of the transformation point and then concentrating on the data translation. There is no need to touch or focus on data that does not need translation. The dataset that needs translation at any interaction point in a process will necessarily be less than the entire dataset, making the management less difficult, occupying fewer resources and being easier to maintain. In the end, representation in any communication medium becomes simple exercises of collection and formatting based on language and use rules.

Breaking the problem down by CoP helps in many ways. First, not all data in one CoP needs to be translated for another CoP. Regardless of an "enterprise" function like risk, that horizontal enterprise function does not need *every* data point that every CoP has. There is a finite universe that any one CoP requires from another CoP. In traditional data management, we have been chasing the false grail of a golden copy of harmonized and agreed-upon terms. Meanwhile, that effort is boiling the ocean in trying to tackle everything and bring all data together in a monolinguistic dictionary.

Next, the interaction between CoPs is more often than not use-case driven. This provides the pragmatic basis for defining the environment, roles, and history of discourse between communities that can frame what the listener is aiming to get and what the speaker is actually providing. Too often when two communities interact, in the search for data individuals look for exact matches first, then tend to accept data that may be "close enough." There is little exploration on why meanings may differ, and if an exact match can be assembled through other data that may not at first seem relevant. Too often, only after things go awry, or there is a fire drill and unrelenting investigation will understanding be found and someone declaring "Oohhhhhh! You're looking for XYZ!" as the penny drops. But this is reactive, and usually by brute force, versus a thorough linguistic investigation occurring during the development process.

Of course, none of this is possible unless you go through the effort of mapping the CoPs that exist, and how they interact in the identified social system. This is, of course, easier said than done. While there may be some alignment with functional or organizational groups, CoPs will be slightly messier. There will be overlapping groups, existing horizontally and vertically. Also, depending on the organization's size, culture, and function, CoPs may be more or less complex.

The most complicating factor is that if one does not belong to a particular CoP, one probably has a level of bias that limits their ability to identify CoPs. We all will come with a bias and are less discerning on how we classify those who are out-group versus in-group members.

So, then, here is an overly simplified checklist to begin:

- Identify CoPs and document using familiar tools.
- Identify, document, and model interaction points between CoPs.

- Focusing on CoP-based data dictionaries, glossaries, or ontologies versus general, broad, or consensus-driven definitions.
- Maintaining ontological models of interactions and translations.
- Include pragmatics-led factors, such as speaker/listener, environment, context, purpose, and so forth within your data modeling discipline.
- Remember that the CoPs can overlap, horizontally and vertically, and are part of larger social systems

CHAPTER 11

Some Final Words

So many exciting things are going on in data and bound to develop in the future. Data is, after all, the output of everything we do. Our personal and professional lives all revolve around data, now more than ever. And the pace at which data comes at us is beyond what we could have imagined 10 years ago, let alone a generation. To help manage it all, we call on technology to store, group, sort, analyze, sift, and curate data. But as we see with social media data, success is hard to come by. Echo chambers form, or we see the erroneous association of irrelevant data, or even worse, relevant data we want to see filtered out.

Meanwhile, search systems like Google have made us feel smarter than ever. We diagnose ourselves on WebMD, find out how to fix a small engine on YouTube, and discover the reasons for the causes of World War I on Wikipedia. And with chatbots powered by LLMs and GPT technologies, we can create drafts or final summary papers on subjects like 17th-century musicians or the evolution of F1 racing.

There is a difference between learning and understanding versus just reading or listening to someone speak on a subject. There is an effort one must put into any endeavor to be able to decipher and comprehend information. Further, even when putting in this effort and reaching a level of true comprehension, this does not make one an expert on the subject. Expertise is gained through continued dedication to that subject, interacting with others, and testing one's knowledge against the community. And even then, most can admit that even the experts can't know everything. This difference gives us a chuckling irony when we experts deem things outside our primary domains to be known or understood because they seem similar or close enough.

There is perhaps an aptitude for learning things close to our expertise, just as one may have a special skill or expertise in learning different languages. But that does not give us expertise in that other skill or language, especially if we do not learn it from the ground up—the foundational principles and building blocks. Understanding data and semantics is a critical skill, but not learning the basics leads to incorrect assertions such as "the primary concern of semantics is to give context."

Lost in the sea of technology are the social pieces necessary for us to consider in data management. Data is not just a language, but data is language. We differentiate data in meaning and use across varied social systems and further diversified by individual Communities of Practice. The challenges speakers of different natural languages face are the same challenges that different CoPs must face in their interactions.

Practitioners in one community who need to interact across community boundaries learn to accommodate by translating names and meanings on the fly. This approach is a standard linguistic method within discourse but requires experience, knowledge, and incorporation of the current environment and context to succeed. This problem is why pragmatics matters—semantics, even with the inclusion of context, does not address the required variables for true accuracy and understanding. Communities will always have language differences, and attempting to solve those differences by assimilation, hegemony, or homogeneity ignores the nature of language and specialization.

Standards exist to solve use-case-specific alignment problems, not to force all things to be homogeneous. There is a balancing act in the creation and application of standards. By their nature, standards tend to become anchors, impacting innovation. Standards can be improperly wielded by vested interests or those in power to curtail competition under the guise of the benefits standards can and do deliver. In many spaces, standards work is opaque and can be biased toward an unintended majority that is not recognized. Because CoPs can exist horizontally and vertically in a matrix, it is possible not to acknowledge an out-group's divergent view. Aligning data standards to the realities of language can boost interoperability and better clarity of understanding.

The power of technology gives false confidence in our ability to solve all our data problems and to give every individual access to all information. But even then, having access to information does not guarantee any expectation of understanding and comprehension. It is not feasible for a single person or community to know or understand everything. But this is essentially the basis for plans regarding data democratization. A CoP should have access to all the necessary information in the language they understand. But providing data to them in a different language, without translation—a pragmatic interpretation of that data—can only lead to errors and misunderstanding.

We should view conflict between CoPs in the light of a sociolinguistic problem. Mutual understanding does not need to lead to data definitions and meaning convergence. Instead, accommodation should happen where appropriate, and we should leverage other language tools focused on translation and preservation of nuance (that supports specialization benefits) to enable interoperability. Newer technologies and methods like data mesh can help with this, yet an understanding of applied linguistics approaches should lead to analysis before solutions.

I wish I could offer a more concrete playbook. But any definitions I come up with to bind specific financial services groupings, those resulting CoPs would necessarily be biased and not encompass all the necessary communities. There is a need for a diverse group of experts to come together and start to provide some attributes on where boundaries should be defined. The less agreement, the better. What is needed is understanding, not harmonization and consensus. If there is disagreement, that is likely the first clue as to where a boundary between communities exist.

Using this as a guide, a foundation, I am hopeful that the data community can come together and look to insert the concepts regarding applied pragmatics and CoP within the data management arena. This will not only necessitate engaging beyond the technology realm but also needs the interoperability between disparate technologies to recognize and express concepts and translate between methodologies.

The data code is complex, ever-evolving, and changing, and we need to stay adaptable and pull from many different disciplines. Only by recognizing differences in language and communities can we bring together the experts needed, recognize the inherent biases, account for them, and perhaps finally begin to crack the data code.

Notes

Chapter 1

1. Haldane, *Towards a common financial language. Speech, Securities Industry and Financial Markets Association (SIFMA) Symposium.*

Chapter 2

1. Lave and Wenger, *Situated learning: Legitimate peripheral participation.*

Chapter 3

1. Workshop Report, *Standards Wars: Myth of Realty? How the forces of competition, convergence and coordination impact standards development*, 2.
2. Ibid, 5.
3. Ibid, 6.
4. Forbes, "Saussure."

Chapter 4

1. Wenger-Trayner, *Communities of Practice and Social Learning Systems: The Career of a Concept.*
2. Robinson, *Understanding the Financial Industry Through Linguistics.*
3. Hall, Smith, and Wicaksono, *Mapping Applied Linguistics*, 2.
4. Ibid, 9.
5. Ibid, 78.
6. Ibid, 80.
7. Hutchby and Wooffitt, *Conversation Analysis.*
8. Bottega and Powell. *Creating a Linchpin for Financial Data: The Need for a Legal Entity Identifier.*

Chapter 5

1. Nouraldeen, *Meaning and Context-Three Different Perspectives*, 13–17.
2. Ibid.
3. Ibid.
4. Nichols, *The Death of Expertise*.
5. Iacozza, *Exploring Social Biases in Language Processing*.
6. Ibid.
7. Bazerman, Loewenstein, and Moore. *Why Good Accountants Do Bad Audits*.
8. Ibid.
9. Pike, Curtis, and Chui, 1413–1431.
10. Kirkpatrick, van Teijlingen, *Lost in Translation: Reflecting on a Model to Reduce Translation and Interpretation Bias*, 25–32. Doi: 10.2174/187 4434600903010025. PMID: 19587795; PMCID: PMC2705066.

Chapter 6

1. Nichols, *The Death of Expertise*.
2. Ibid.
3. Ibid.
4. Ibid.
5. Ibid.
6. Bellec, *What Is Data Democratization and Why Is It Important?*
7. Bunting, *From Silos to Collaboration*.
8. Wingfield, *Data Democratization: Promise vs Reality*.
9. Bellec, *What Is Data Democratization and Why Is It Important?*
10. Thereaux.
11. Langefors, *Essays on Infology*, 159.
12. Ibid.
13. Abbas and Michael, *Socio-Technical Theory: A Review*.

Chapter 7

1. Nouraldeen, *Meaning and Context-Three Different Perspectives*, 13–17.
2. Ibid.
3. Ibid.

Chapter 8

1. MacMahon, *Stylistics: Pragmatic Approaches*, 232–236.

Chapter 9

1. Sassure, Chapter 2.
2. Ibid.
3. Codd, *A Relational Model of Data for Large Shared Data Banks*, 377–387.
4. Langefors, "Essays on Infology."
5. Dehghani, *Data Mesh; Delivering Data Driven Value at Scale.*
6. Ibid.
7. Ibid.
8. Ibid.
9. Ibid.
10. Willis, *The Ultimate Guide to Data Lineage.*
11. Steenbeek.
12. Garten, Kennedy, Sagae, et al, *Measuring the Importance of Context When Modeling Language Comprehension*, 480–492.
13. Iacozza, *Exploring Social Biases in Language Processing.*
14. Requejo and Dolores, *The Role of Context in Word Meaning Construction: A Case Study*, 169–173.
15. Ibid.
16. Ibid.
17. Nouraldeen, *Meaning and Context-Three Different Perspectives*, 13–17.
18. Tselova, *Why Data Storytelling Is Important for Your Business.*
19. Davenport, *Why Data Storytelling Is So Important—and Why We're So Bad at It.*

References

Abbas, R. and K. Michael. *Socio-Technical Theory: A Review*, ed. S. Papagiannidis (TheoryHub Book, 2023). Available at http://open.ncl.ac.uk / ISBN: 9781739604400.

Bazerman, M., G. Loewenstein, and D. Moore. "Why Good Accountants Do Bad Audits." *Harvard Business Review* (2002). Accessed September 5, 2023. www.andrew.cmu.edu/user/gl20/GeorgeLoewenstein/Papers_files/pdf/WhyGoodAccountants.pdf.

Bellec, Anne-Claire. "What Is Data Democratization and Why Is It Important? Accessed August 23, 2023. www.opendatasoft.com/en/blog/what-is-data -democratization/.

Bellec, Anne-Claire. "What Is Data Democratization and Why Is It Important? Accessed August 23, 2023. www.opendatasoft.com/en/blog/what-is-data -democratization/.

Bottega, John, A. and Linda. F. Powell. *Creating a Linchpin for Financial Data: The Need for a Legal Entity Identifier* (December 10, 2010). Available at SSRN: https://ssrn.com/abstract=1723298 or http://dx.doi.org/10.2139/ssrn.1723298.

Bunting, David. "From Silos to Collaboration." Accessed August 23, 2023. www.chaossearch.io/blog/product-analytics-data-democratization.

Codd, E.F. "A Relational Model of Data for Large Shared Data Banks." *Commun.* ACM 13, no.6 (June 1970), 377–387. https://doi.org/10.1145/362384.362685.

Davenport, Tom. "Why Data Storytelling Is So Important—and Why We're So Bad at It." Accessed November3, 2023. www2.deloitte.com/xe/en/insights/topics/analytics/data-driven-storytelling.html.

Dehghani, Z. *Data Mesh; Delivering Data Driven Value at Scale*. O'Reilly. doi: 10.2174/1874434600903010025. PMID: 19587795; PMCID: PMC2705066.

Garten, J., B. Kennedy, K. Sagae, et al. "Measuring the Importance of Context When Modeling Language Comprehension." *Behav Res* 51 (2019), 480–492. https://doi.org/10.3758/s13428-019-01200-w.

Haldane, A.G. March 14, 2012. Bank for International Settlements. "Towards a common financial language. Speech, Securities Industry and Financial Markets Association (SIFMA) Symposium." New York. Accessed August 2019. www.bis.org/review/r120315g.pdf.

Hall, C., P. Smith, and R. Wicaksono. *Mapping Applied Linguistics* (New York, NY, Routledge, 2010), 2.

Ibid, 9.

Ibid, 78.

Ibid, 80.

Hutchby, Ian and Robin Wooffitt. *Conversation Analysis* (Polity, 2008).

Iacozza, Sara. "Exploring Social Biases in Language Processing." Doctoral Thesis. August 24, 2023. https://pure.mpg.de/rest/items/item_3195118_4/component/file_3236505/content.

Kirkpatrick, P. and E. Teijlingen. "Lost in Translation: Reflecting on a Model to Reduce Translation and Interpretation Bias." *The Open Nursing Journal* 3(June 23, 2009): 25–32.

Langefors, B. *Essays on Infology* (Chartwell-Bratt, 1995), 159.

Ibid.   https://link.springer.com/content/pdf/10.1007%2F978-3-642-03757-3_11.pdf.

Lave, J. and E. Wenger. *Situated Learning: Legitimate Peripheral Participation*. Cambridge University Press, 1991. https://doi.org/10.1017/CBO9780511815355

MacMahon, B. "Stylistics: Pragmatic Approaches."In *Encyclopedia of Language & Linguistics*, ed. Keith Brown (Elsevier, 2006), 232–236.

Nichols, Tom. *The Death of Expertise*. Oxford University Press, 2017

Nouraldeen, Abdullah Soliman. "Meaning and Context-Three Different Perspectives." *British Journal of English Linguistics* 3, no. 2 (May, 2015): 13–17. Accessed February 16, 2023. www.eajournals.org/wp-content/uploads/Meaning-and-Context-Three-Different-Perspectives..pdf.

Pike, B.J., M.B. Curtis, and L. Chui. "How Does an Initial Expectation Bias Influence Auditors' Application and Performance of Analytical Procedures?" *The Accounting Review* 88, no. 4(2013): 1413–1431.

Porto Requejo, and Maria Dolores. "The Role of Context in Word Meaning Construction: A Case Study." *International Journal of English Studies* 7, no. 1 (2007), 169–173.

Robinson, R. *Understanding the Financial Industry Through Linguistics* (Business Expert Press, 2021).

Saussure. Chapter 2. Accessed August 24, 2023. http://mforbes.sites.gettysburg.edu/cims226/wp-content/uploads/2018/09/Week-2a-Ferdinand-de-Saussure.pdf.

Steenbeek, I. Accessed August 31, 2023. https://datacrossroads.nl/2018/12/16/data-management-maturity-models-a-comparative-analysis/.

Thereaux, Olivier. Accessed August 23, 2023. www.youtube.com/watch?v=kBGbCpGBXo0.

Tselova, Simone. "Why Data Storytelling Is Important for Your Business." Accessed November 3, 2023. https://flourish.studio/blog/importance-of -data-storytelling/.

Wenger-Trayner, Etienne. *Communities of Practice and Social Learning Systems: The Career of a Concept.* 2010. 10.1007/978-1-84996-133-2_11.

Willis, Glenn. The Ultimate Guide to Data Lineage. Accessed August 31, 2023. www.montecarlodata.com/blog-data-lineage/.

Wingfield, R. "Data Democratization: Promise vs Reality." Accessed Augst 23, 2023. www.actian.com/blog/data-management/data-democratization -promise-vs-reality/.

Workshop Report, *Standards Wars: Myth of Realty? How the Forces of Competition, Convergence and Coordination Impact Standards Development*, May 11, 2011, 2.

Ibid, 5.

Ibid, 6.

About the Author

Rich Robinson is a senior executive with 30 years of experience across operations and technology functions in the financial industry. He has worked throughout the front, mid, and back offices at major global custodian banks, brokerages, and industry utilities, leading transformative projects in data, operations workflow, and messaging.

For over 25 years, Rich, in addition to his full-time jobs, has been heavily involved in the industry as an active participant in key working groups related to international data and messaging standards, including ISITC, FISD, EDM Council, ISO, ANSI/X9, ISDA, and SIFMA. He cofounded the first group on Unique Instrument Identification in 2000 and was a primary participant in the Best Practice work for ISO15022. He was a Convener for the ISO Study Group on CFI's and UPI and led the ISO Working Group on the Unique Transaction Identifier standard. Rich is on the Board of Directors of ISITC, serves as Chair, is lead Sherpa for the Asia Pacific Finance Forum Financial Market Infrastructure Workstream on behalf of the Asian Business Advisory Council to the region's Finance Ministers, and is co-vice Convener of the Registration Management Group (RMG) for ISO 20022.

A regular speaker at conferences, he has been published in the *Journal of Securities Operations and Custody, Waters, and Inside Reference Data*, among other global financial services publications. His 2018 paper, "A linguistics approach to solving financial services standardization," introduces the innovative idea of using applied linguistics to guide standards development and regulatory decisions and was published in the *Journal of Financial Markets Infrastructure*. It was the original basis for his first book, *Understanding the Financial Industry Through Linguistics*.

Richard is currently Chief Strategist for Standards and Open Data at Bloomberg LLP. He works globally with regulators, legislators, and industry leaders to address data and standards issues to create more efficient and transparent markets. He holds an MBA in Organizational Behavior and Information Technology from NYU's Stern School and a BS in Industrial

Management with a concentration in Management Information Systems from Carnegie Mellon University.

Rich, in his spare time, plays soccer (supports Fulham, NYRB, and the Riverhounds), surfs (yes, East Coast USA), snowboards, gardens, plays guitar (poorly), and volunteers as a mentor for students and veterans entering the business world. He also writes some fiction and poetry. He has three adult boys, Dylan, Kyle, and Gavin, of whom he is extremely proud, and who mean the world to him. His wife, Lisa, is a retired eighth grade History teacher, a constant source of inspiration, and love of his life. In addition to the boys, Lisa and Rich also care for a menagerie of three rescue dogs and a rescue cat.

Index

Aggregate domain approach, 94–95
American Nation Standards Institute
(ANSI), 16
Applied linguistics, 23–44, 115
Artificial intelligence (AI), 105–114
Austin, J. L., 38
Autonomous cars, 111

BARC Business Intelligence and
Analytics Survey, 51
Berardino, J., 57
Bias, 50–53
context influence, 54
in-group, out-group, 53–54
in reading data, 56–59
in stored data, 55–56
Big data, 86, 90–92, 109
Boyce-Codd Normal Form (BCNF),
85
Bunting, D., 66

Cajun creole, 28
Capability Maturity Model
Integration (CMMI), 102–
103
Čapek, K., 109
Central Bank Digital Coins (CBDC),
124
ChatGPT, 108–113
Cloud Data Management Capabilities
(CDMC), 103
Codd, E. F., normal forms, 84–85
Common standards, 3–4, 11–22
Communities of Practice (CoPs), 2–5,
5f, 7–9, 13–15, 17, 18, 20–
22, 29–31, 35, 37–41, 44, 46,
48, 51–56, 58–59, 66, 68, 69,
71, 74, 75, 78–83, 87, 93–95,
98–99, 104, 107, 112, 114,
120–125, 127–128, 130–131,
134–141, 144–145
Computational linguistics, 115

Conduct bias, 51
Confirmation bias, 51, 57, 117
Consumer-aligned approach, 94
Context, 46–50
Context matters, 112
COVID-19 pandemic, 86
Creole languages, 27–28

Data
analytics, 99–100
capture, 95–97
democratization, 64–70
lineage and tracking, 98–99
management and governance, 81,
100–104
marts and lakehouses, 91–92
mesh, 92–95
quality control, 97–98
steward, 121–123
storage, 83–92
storytelling, 116–121
structured, 91
unstructured, 90
visualization, 116–119
warehouse, 90–91
Data Administration Management
Association (DAMA), 101–
102
Data Management Body of
Knowledge book (DMBOK),
101–102
Data Management Capability
Assessment Model (DCAM),
103, 130
Data Management Maturity Model
(DMM), 102, 103
Davenport, T., 119
Dehghani, Z., 93–95
Delivery order, 21
Dialect languages, 3, 24–27
Dick, P. K., 109
Dillinger, M., 124

Direct speech, 49–50
Discourse analysis, 37–39
Dog, concept of, 13–15
Domain archetypes, 94–95
Domain-driven design (DDD), 93
Dunning-Kruger effect, 61

EDMC, 103
EDM Council, 102, 103
ELIZA, 106
English language, 29–30, 122
Epistemic context, 47
Exchange-traded funds (ETFs), 29
Execution, 20–21, 50, 76, 137
Expertise, 52–55, 61–63, 89, 98, 143
EXtensible Markup Language (XML),
    11
Extract, transform, and load (ETL)
    process, 96

Fifth Normal Form (5NF), 85
2008 financial crisis, 42–44
Financial industry, 2, 133
Financial language, 23, 31–32, 42
Financial services, 4–5, 18, 29–31,
    36, 38, 41, 45, 55, 57, 58,
    75, 95, 103, 123, 127, 131,
    133, 145
First Normal Form (1NF), 84
Fourth Normal Form (4NF), 85

Garbage in, garbage out (GIGO),
    113, 114
Granular data, 71–76, 82–83
Greek language, 30

Haldane, A. G., 1

Indirect speech, 49–50
Information Systems Audit and
    Control Association (ISACA),
    102
ISO7775, 88
ISO15022, 88

Jargon languages, 3, 24–28, 55

Kaku, M., 108, 111

Language(s), 29–32
    child's, 35
    creole, 27–28
    and dialect, 3, 24–27
    difference, 4, 5, 25, 27, 40, 44, 66,
        110, 121, 136–138, 144
    English, 29–30, 122
    jargon, 3, 24–28, 55
    problems, 23–41
    repair and accommodation,
        40–41
    right vs. wrong, 34
    translation, 122–123
    written and stored data, 35–37
Large language models (LLM), 108,
    112, 127, 143
Lave, J., 7
Linguistic diversity, 1
Linguistic knowledge gap, 114–116
Linguistics and applied linguistics,
    23–44
Long short-term memory (LSTM)
    networks, 112

Machine learning (ML), 105–114
MacMahon, B., 77
Master data management, 95, 100–
    104, 113
Matrix organizations, 132
Maturity model, 101
McWhorter, J., The Atlantic, 24
Middleware, 58, 87–89, 129
MiFID, 32
MiFIR, 32
Mutual intelligibility, 24–26, 30

Natural language processing (NLP),
    106–107
Nonfungible tokens (NFTs), 124
Normalization, 84–85
NoSQL, 86
Nouraldeen, 48, 116

Opendatasoft blog, 66
Order, 20–21

Payments Market Practice Group
    (PMPG), 41

Personally identifiable information
(PII), 65, 93
Physical context, 47
Pidgin languages, 27
Pragmatics, 38, 77–80, 112, 116,
120, 121, 127–141, 145

Relational database management
systems (RDBM), 84–86
Reported speech, 49–50
Requejo, P., 114, 115
Rules-based NLP, 106–107

Sangani, S., 109, 110
Saussure, 20, 82, 83
Second Normal Form (2NF), 84
Securities Market Practice Group
(SMPG), 41
Semantics, 45–59
Silos, 136–137
Slang, 26
Small and medium enterprises (SME),
52–53
Social context, 47
Software Engineering Institute (SEI),
102, 103
Sommelier, 33–34
Source-aligned data, 94
Spaghetti web, 87–89

Standards, 3–4, 11–22, 144
Star Wars, 8
Statistical NLP, 107
Steenbeek, I., 101
Storage, data, 83–92
Storytelling, 116–121
Structured Query Language (SQL),
85–86

Taylor, P., 86
Technology, 81–83, 144–145
AI and machine learning, 105–114
linguistic knowledge gap, 114–116
storage, 83–92
taxonomy, 123–125
See also Data
Third Normal Form (3NF), 84–85
Trade changes, concept of, 18–22,
71–72, 74, 76, 78–80, 137
Transformation, data cleansing,
96–97
Translator's bias, 58
Transportation types, 123

Weinreich, M., 25
Wenger-Trayner, E., 7, 30, 31
Why Good Accountants Do
Bad Audits (Bazerman,
Loewenstein, and Moore), 57

www.ingramcontent.com/pod-product-compliance
Lightning Source LLC
Chambersburg PA
CBHW061313220326
41599CB00026B/4864